CAPITAL MARKETS AND CORPORATE GOVERNANCE IN JAPAN, GERMANY AND THE UNITED STATES

Germany, Japan and the United States are the world's three largest economies. Despite their common economic success, companies in these three countries operate within rather unique financial systems. Germany's financial system is characterized by weak corporate stock and bond markets, strong universal banks and high levels of ownership concentration. Keiretsu organizations—large corporate networks—are the center of Japan's financial system. The US system is dominated by strong capital market forces. These differences raise various questions. Why did financial keiretsu develop in Japan, but not in Germany and the United States? Why is bank intermediation more dominant in Germany and Japan than in the United States? What are the advantages and disadvantages of each system?

This study answers these and related questions. It explains capital market intermediation, holding companies, multidivisional organizations, financial keiretsu and LBO associations as organizational responses to capital market inefficiencies. Country-specific responses are described as a consequence of country-specific financial regulations. Each regulatory regime results in specific capital market inefficiencies. The book contains a comprehensive description of German, Japanese and US regulations. Comparative capital market and corporate data highlight the major strengths and weaknesses of each system.

Helmut M. Dietl is Professor of Organization and International Management at the University of Paderborn, Germany. He is co-editor of the book series *NIE—New Institutional Economics*, author of *Institutions and Time* (in German), and co-author of *Organization—An Economic Perspective* (in German and Japanese). He has contributed to refereed journals and published in four languages.

ROUTLEDGE STUDIES IN THE
MODERN WORLD ECONOMY

CAPITAL MARKETS AND CORPORATE GOVERNANCE IN JAPAN, GERMANY AND THE UNITED STATES

Organizational Response to Market Inefficiencies

Helmut M. Dietl

London and New York

First published 1998
by Routledge
11 New Fetter Lane, London EC4P 4EE

Simultaneously published in the USA and Canada
by Routledge
29 West 35th Street, New York, NY 10001

© 1998 Helmut M. Dietl

Typeset in Garamond by Routledge
Printed and bound in Great Britain by
T J International Ltd, Padstow, Cornwall

British Library Cataloguing in Publication Data
A catalogue record for this book is available from the
British Library

Library of Congress Cataloguing in Publication Data
Dietl, Helmut Max
Capital markets and corporate governance in
Japan, Germany and the United
States: organizational response to market inefficiencies/
Helmut M. Dietl.
Includes bibliographical references and index.
1. Capital market–United States. 2. Capital market–Germany.
3. Capital market–Japan. 4. Corporate governance–United States.
5. Corporate governance–Germany. 6. Corporate governance–Japan.
I. Title.
HG4910. D53 1998
97–21404
332', 041–dc21
CIP

ISBN 0–415–17188–1

CONTENTS

ILLUSTRATIONS

FIGURES

TABLES

ACKNOWLEDGEMENTS

During my research I have benefited greatly from the advice of Franklin Allen, Harald Baum, Gary Gorton, Mitsuhiro Hirata, Akihiro Koyama, Shuichi Manchu, Arnold Picot, Ralf Reichwald, Bernd Rudolph, Ekkehard Wenger, Oliver E. Williamson and Wei Zhang. I want to thank the Institute of Management, Innovation and Organization at the University of California, Berkeley; the Finance Department of the Wharton School of Business, University of Pennsylvania; the Institute of Business Research at Hitotsubashi University, Tokyo; and their respective directors David J. Teece, Richard E. Kihlstrom and Ikujiro Nonaka for supporting my research in the United States and Japan. I am grateful to Yufeng Chen, who typed most of the manuscript, Andreas Schnitzer, who helped to create the illustrations, and Angela Shelley, who edited the manuscript.

Finally, financial support from the Deutsche Forschungsgemein-schaft (German Research Foundation) is gratefully acknowledged.

INTRODUCTION

Germany, Japan, and the United States represent the world's three largest economies. Despite their common economic success, German, Japanese and US companies operate within rather unique financial systems. Germany's financial system is dominated by large universal banks. Markets for corporate stocks and corporate bonds are not well developed. Corporate ownership is highly concentrated. Nonfinancial enterprises are the most important group of shareholders.

Banks play a dominant role within the Japanese financial system. Although they are not allowed to acquire more than 5 percent of a corporation's outstanding shares, Japanese banks own more than one-fifth of all Japanese stocks. They are the center of keiretsu organizations—large financial networks based on cross shareholdings, short-term credits, long-term commitments, director interlinkages and inter-firm trading.

The US capital market is well developed. Bank intermediation is less important than in Germany and Japan. Corporate ownership is highly fragmented. Private households constitute the largest group of shareholders, owning about three-quarters of all US stocks. Despite the strength of US stock and bond markets, multidivisional organization has become popular in the United States. Like their German and Japanese counterparts, many US corporations have created internal capital markets by adopting a multidivisional structure. Contrary to German and Japanese multidivisional corporations, however, US conglomerates became the target of leveraged buyouts. During the 1980s a large number of US corporations were restructured as a result of hostile takeovers.

These differences raise various questions. For example, why are holding companies popular in Germany? Why did financial keiretsu develop in Japan, but not in Germany and the United States? Why is bank intermediation more dominant in Germany and Japan than in

1

the United States? Why are US and Japanese capital markets more developed than the German capital market? Why are multidivisional organizations common in all three countries? Why did leveraged buyouts occur in the United States, but not in Germany and Japan?

This book tries to answer these and related questions in terms of economic efficiency. Unintermediated capital markets, intermediated capital markets, holding companies, multidivisional organizations, LBO associations and financial keiretsu are regarded as alternative modes of capital allocation and corporate governance. If capital markets were the efficient mode of capital allocation and corporate governance under all circumstances, the prevailing organizational variety could not be explained in efficiency terms. Moreover, the organizational variety could not survive in a competitive environment.

The survival and economic success of alternative modes of capital allocation and corporate governance suggest that capital markets are not efficient under all circumstances. In this case, holding companies, multidivisional organizations, financial keiretsu, etc., could be interpreted as an organizational response to capital market inefficiencies.

In order to identify potential capital market inefficiencies, Chapter 1 develops a theoretical framework for comparative efficiency analysis of alternative modes of capital allocation and corporate governance. Potential capital market inefficiencies are determined by three factors: capital market regulations; the efficiency features of alternative modes of capital allocation and corporate governance; and the characteristics of the underlying investment relation.

Capital market regulations determine the rights and obligations of capital market participants. Different regulatory environments may result in different capital market imperfections. For example, effective prohibition of insider trading may impair the ability of the price mechanism to aggregate and transmit insider knowledge, whereas anti-takeover regulations eliminate the disciplinary effects of an active market for corporate control. Including the regulatory environment as a determinant of capital market imperfections is the first of three basic foundations of the comparative organizational analysis within Chapter 1.

Not all capital market imperfections result in capital market inefficiencies. Capital market imperfections are a necessary but not sufficient condition for capital market inefficiencies. This is the second basic foundation of comparative organizational analysis. An imperfect mode of economic organization must be regarded as efficient as long as there is no alternative mode of economic organization which does not suffer from the same imperfections.

Imperfections are defined in absolute terms, inefficiencies in relative terms. Imperfections describe the differences between a theoretical ideal and real-world modes of economic organization. Inefficiencies describe differences among real-world modes of economic organization.

Relative efficiency among alternative modes of capital allocation and corporate governance cannot be defined in general terms. Relative efficiency may vary from case to case. While unintermediated capital markets may be the efficient mode of capital allocation and corporate governance for a certain kind of investment relation, holding companies or financial keiretsu may be the efficient organizational mode for another kind of investment relation. This theoretical concept of situational efficiency is the third basic foundation of the comparative organizational analysis in Chapter 1.

Based on these foundations, Chapter 1 introduces a theoretical framework which explains capital market intermediation, holding companies, multidivisional organization, financial keiretsu and LBO associations as organizational responses to capital market inefficiencies. Country-specific organizational responses to capital market inefficiencies are described as a consequence of country-specific capital market regulations.

The theoretical framework is built on

1 the introduction of investment relations as the basic unit of analysis
2 a comparative efficiency criterion
3 the identification of the relevant dimensions of investment relations
4 a classification of alternative regulatory environments
5 an extensive analysis of the comparative efficiency features of alternative modes of capital allocation and corporate governance, and
6 a discriminating efficiency match.

Chapter 2 reports empirical evidence from Germany, Japan and the United States. The empirical analysis is based on a comprehensive description of country-specific capital market regulations; comparative capital market data which reflect the relative strengths and weaknesses of the German, Japanese, and US capital markets; and a statistical test of the hypotheses developed in Chapter 1.

1

THEORETICAL FRAMEWORK

The objective of this chapter is to develop a theoretical framework which explains the prevailing variety of organizational modes of capital allocation and corporate governance in terms of comparative organizational efficiency. The chapter is divided under six main headings:

1 introducing the investment relation as the basic unit of analysis
2 defining investment relation costs as the comparative efficiency criterion
3 identifying of the relevant dimensions of an investment relation
4 classifying of alternative regulatory environments
5 characterizing of alternative organizational modes of capital allocation and corporate governance
6 matching of each type of investment relation in an efficiency discriminating manner with a particular organizational mode of capital allocation and corporate governance.

INVESTMENT RELATION

The investment relation is the basic unit of analysis. It consists of at least two parties: an investor who provides capital and a firm which uses capital for investment purposes. In exchange for the provision of capital, investors receive contingent ownership and decision rights. In states of solvency, for example, the suppliers of equity will retain the decision rights over the firm's assets while the suppliers of debt will receive pre-specified interest and principal payments. In case of default, on the other hand, the decision rights over the firm's remaining assets will be transferred from the suppliers of equity to the suppliers of debt.

Financial intermediation transforms single-stage investment relations into complex multiple-stage investment relations. Consider, for example, the case of bank intermediation. If investors prefer to deposit their money into savings accounts instead of buying corporate bonds, a two-stage investment relation will be established. The bank functions as an intermediate agent. It generates funds from the savings sector and provides capital in form of bank loans to the industry sector.

INVESTMENT RELATION COSTS

Establishing and governing an investment relation results in investment relation costs. This cost category consists of misallocation and governance costs. Misallocation costs represent the economic disadvantages which arise whenever scarce capital is not allocated to its highest yield use.

The expected value of an investment portfolio $E(V_p)$ is a function of the portfolio's expected return r_p and the portfolio's assumed risk σ_p:

$$E(V_p) = E[V(r_p, \sigma_p)]\qquad(1.1)$$

Each investor i will generate portfolio-specific return expectations and risk assumptions according to his or her personal knowledge set θ_i:

$$r_{p_i} = r_p(\theta_i)\qquad(1.2)$$

$$[\sigma_{p_i} = \sigma_p(\theta_i)\qquad(1.3)$$

Each individual knowledge set θ_i may be described as a function of the accurate knowledge set θ_a and an error term ε_i:

$$\theta_i = \theta_a + \varepsilon_i\qquad(1.4)$$

Using equations (1.2) and (1.3), equation (1.1) may be transformed into:

$$E(V_{p_i}) = E[V_p(\theta_i)']\qquad(1.1')$$

According to equation (1.1') the expected value which is assigned to an investment portfolio p by an investor i is solely a function of the investor's knowledge set θ_i.

As depicted in Figure 1.1, inaccurate knowledge may cause an investor to over- or underestimate the expected value of investment portfolios.[1] Consequently, inaccurate knowledge may lead to capital misallocation. Due to imperfect knowledge, investor i assigns the highest expected value of all available investment opportunities to portfolio p_i. Accurate knowledge (θ_a) reveals that investor i overstates the expected value of portfolio pi. The accurate expected value of investment portfolio p_i is $E(V_{p_i}*)$, which is much lower than the accurate expected value of the optimal portfolio $E(V_{p_a}*)$. In this simple example which consists of only one investor, the misallocation costs are defined as the difference between $E(V_{p_a}*)$ and $E(V_{p_i}*)$.

Note here that accurate knowledge is not perfect knowledge. In the case of perfect knowledge, an investor would know the future cashflows of all available investment projects, whereas the term "accurate knowledge" is used here to express that an investor correctly estimates the expected return and risk of available investment portfolios. In short, perfect knowledge implies knowing the future state of the world, accurate knowledge implies knowing possible future states of the world and their respective probabilities. In the extreme case of perfect knowledge, there would be no need for risk diversification.

In the preceding paragraphs, governance problems have been ignored. Misallocation costs have been calculated under assumption

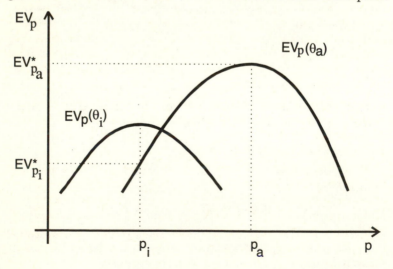

Figure 1.1 Expected value of investment portfolios under accurate and inaccurate knowledge

6

that corporate executives always act in the investors' best interest. Since this assumption cannot be sustained in the real world, governance costs are introduced as the second component of investment relation costs.

Governance costs include all economic disadvantages which arise when both sides of an investment relation, investors on the one and corporate executives on the other, pursue conflicting goals, i.e.when corporate executives do not automatically act in the investors' best interest. While investors seek to maximize the value of their investments, executives may try to enhance their status, leisure time, or personal wealth at the investors' expense. This potential conflict of interests will result in governance costs, which are composed of agency costs and nondiversification costs. Agency costs include signaling, screening, monitoring, and residual costs.[2]

Nondiversification costs represent the economic disadvantages of holding an undiversified investment portfolio. Investors who forego optional levels of risk diversification in order to improve corporate governance expose themselves to unsystematic risk. The economic disadvantages of this kind of risk exposure have to be taken into account as part of the overall governance costs.

Signaling costs are the only governance costs which are directly borne by the firm. Investors expose themselves to potential appropriation hazards when entering an investment relation, because corporate executives may act opportunistically and use the investors' capital in a sub-optimal or even value-destroying fashion. Since this behavioral uncertainty may result in increasing capital costs and credit rationing, firms whose executives intend to behave honestly possess strong economic incentives to provide potential investors with credible commitments[3] in order to signal high degrees of asset quality, behavioral reliability and trustworthiness. Signaling costs represent the economic burden which is incurred by a firm when providing potential investors with credible commitments.

Screening costs result from the information activities which are undertaken by investors in an attempt to discern the characteristics of a firm and its executives prior to entering into an investment relation. Monitoring costs are the *ex post* equivalent to *ex ante* screening costs. Monitoring costs result from information activities and disciplinary measures which are undertaken by investors during an investment relation in order to detect and sanction opportunism.

Despite signaling, screening and monitoring activities, discretionary freedoms may remain which can be exploited by corporate executives in an opportunistic manner. The resulting economic disadvantages of this behavioral uncertainty are subsumed under the term "residual costs."

There is a trade-off relation among the four categories of governance costs. Higher costs in one category will result in lower costs in one or more of the other categories. For example, an investor who incurs higher screening costs may be able to reduce the amount of monitoring and residual costs; saving on signaling, screening, and monitoring costs will lead to an increase in residual costs.

So far, governance costs have been described from the perspective of a single-stage investment relation. In the case of financial intermediation, governance costs may arise at each stage. From the investor's viewpoint, intermediary agencies may behave opportunistically and therefore have to be screened and monitored, whereas the agency itself may incur signaling costs to reduce information asymmetries or provide credible commitments. From the firm's viewpoint, intermediary agencies represent investors, and therefore will incur screening, monitoring, and nondiversification costs.

According to this systematization, inefficient risk diversification may be subsumed under misallocation and nondiversification costs. To the extent that inefficient risk diversification is the result of inaccurate risk expectations, it is part of the misallocation costs; to the extent that it is the result of governance-induced ownership concentration, its economic disadvantage is expressed by nondiversification costs as part of the total governance costs.

Although the costs of quantifying investment relation costs are prohibitively high in most empirical situations, the level of investment relation costs is a useful criterion for the purpose of assessing the comparative efficiency of alternative modes of capital allocation and corporate governance. Just as a person's relative height can often be assessed without a yardstick, alternative modes of capital allocation and corporate governance can be ranked based on a comparative analysis of investment relation costs. In addition, investment relation costs may be measured indirectly if a statistical correlation between the amount of investment relation costs and quantifiable characteristics of an investment relation can be established.

RELEVANT DIMENSIONS OF INVESTMENT RELATIONS

Organizational modes of capital allocation and corporate governance differ primarily with regard to

1 the type and amount of knowledge which they are able to generate and use during the process of capital allocation, and

2 their ability to reduce governance costs.

As has been indicated above, the level of risk diversification which is attained by an organizational mode does not represent a separate feature, but rather is covered by these two features. Inefficient risk diversification results either from a lack of knowledge or from ownership concentration in response to agency problems. Lack of knowledge will result in misallocation costs; ownership concentration in response to agency problems will result in governance costs.

In order to match investment relations with organizational modes of capital allocation and corporate governance in an efficiency discriminating manner, investment relations have to be dimensionalized along those characteristics which reflect the type and amount of knowledge necessary to allocate capital efficiently, and the type and magnitude of governance problems associated with the investment relation. The respective characteristics are industry maturity and investment plasticity.

Industry maturity

The level of industry maturity describes an industry's current state of development. Mature industries operate in a relatively stable or at least predictable environment. Their markets and products are well developed. There is little scope for market expansion. Firms which succeed in increasing their market share do so primarily at the expense of their competitors. Product improvement proceeds gradually. Innovations are incremental rather than revolutionary.

It usually takes several decades until an industry reaches maturity. The relatively long history of mature industries provides industry insiders with large amounts of investment-relevant knowledge and experience. Combined with a relatively stable and predictable industry environment, this knowledge and experience enables industry insiders to accurately estimate the expected return and risk of new investments within the industry. Examples of those which have reached high levels of maturity are the steel, automobile, and brewing industries.

Immature industries operate in an unstable and unpredictable environment. Neither markets nor products are well developed. Innovations often redefine the structure of the entire industry. New competitors are attracted by low entry barriers. Most companies within the industry balance on a thin line between growth and bankruptcy. The inherent danger of economic failure casts its shadow on the potential of industry success and market expansion. While some immature industries may succeed, others will disappear.

The relatively short and turbulent history of immature industries prevents industry insiders from acquiring confidential investment-relevant knowledge and experience. Even if industry insiders succeeded in acquiring historical experience, the unstable and unpredictable industry environment would hinder them in estimating the expected return and risk of new investments within immature industries more accurately than outsiders.

At their current stage, biotechnology and telecommunications represent immature industries. The example of the telecommunications industry reveals that some industries may remain at an immature level over a longer period of time. In this industry, ongoing technological innovation and fundamental political changes (e.g. deregulation, privatization) have created an unstable and rather unpredictable environment over many years.

The attributable level of industry maturity describes the potential misallocation problems which are associated with an investment relation. Efficient capital allocation within immature industries requires different types of knowledge than it does within mature industries. Consequently, dimensionalizing investment relations along attributable levels of industry maturity reduces the complexity of determining the efficiency of alternative modes of capital allocation.

Investment plasticity

The term "investment plasticity" was introduced by Alchian and Woodward (1987: 115–17). The degree of investment plasticity is determined by two factors: the range of decisions within which an agent may choose, and the level of information asymmetry between principals and agents.

A wide range of choice options is a necessary but not a sufficient condition for high levels of investment plasticity. A wide range of options combined with symmetric information does not translate into a high level of investment plasticity. Consider, for example, the case of mutual funds. Fund managers usually enjoy a wide range of investment options. Nevertheless, the degree of investment plasticity is relatively low, because investment company regulations reduce potential information asymmetries by forcing investment companies to record and disclose all market transactions. Consequently, investors are able to observe the actions of fund managers at almost no cost.

A wide range of choice options combined with substantial information asymmetries, on the other hand, results in high degrees of investment plasticity. High degrees of investment plasticity expose investors to severe governance problems. Unless agents provide credible commitments, principals must decide whether to invest considerable amounts of time, effort, and money into screening and monitoring activities and to forego an optimal level of risk diversification, or to incur high residual costs. Either way, governance costs will be substantial. In some cases they may even reach prohibitively high levels. Financial intermediation may overcome the resulting inefficiencies. However, each intermediary stage has to be carefully analyzed, because it may be a source of additional plasticity, and as such compound rather than resolve governance problems.

High degrees of investment plasticity are usually encountered in those industries which depend heavily upon human skills, intellect and creativity. Architecture, education, engineering, fashion design and software production provide illuminating examples. Research laboratories, design studios and human capital are further examples of highly plastic investments.

Limited choice options result in a low degree of investment plasticity. Investments which restrict agents to a very limited scope of actions do not cause severe governance problems. Consider, for example, an investment into a steel mill or a power plant. Technological rigidity leaves agents with little room for discretionary behavior. Investors do not have to incur high governance costs in order to restrain opportunism. Gold mines, assembly lines, railroads and oil pipelines are further examples of rather implastic investments.

The degree of investment plasticity reveals the potential governance problems which are associated with an investment relation. Implastic investments require different governance structures than plastic investments. Dimensionalizing investment relations along the attributable degree of investment plasticity reduces the complexity of determining the efficiency of alternative modes of corporate governance.

11

CLASSIFICATION OF ALTERNATIVE REGULATORY ENVIRONMENTS

Alternative regulatory environments may be classified along the following dimensions:

1. accounting, disclosure and auditing regulation
2. regulation of insider trading
3. regulation of market manipulation
4. (anti-) takeover regulation
5. diversification requirements
6. restriction of universal banking.

Accounting, disclosure and auditing regulation

These regulations determine the extent of information asymmetries between corporate insiders and outsiders. Strict accounting, disclosure and auditing rules facilitate corporate governance by corporate outsiders, discourage ownership concentration, enhance risk diversification and promote the participation of large numbers of investors in capital market transactions. Weak accounting, disclosure and auditing rules, on the other hand, increase the costs of outside corporate governance, promote ownership concentration, and discourage outsiders from participating in capital market transactions.

Strict accounting, disclosure and auditing regulations reduce the information asymmetries between corporate insiders and outsiders. Corporate insiders are forced to publish accurate investment-relevant information. Well-defined and well-enforced accounting, disclosure and auditing standards reduce the costs of information interpretation. Assessing a corporation's financial performance and economic perspective does not require advanced accounting skills. Investment-relevant information has to be disclosed in a timely, understandable and comparable fashion. Outside investors who want to invest in corporate governance do not have to incur prohibitively high information costs.

Under strict accounting, disclosure and auditing rules, large and active investors[4] no longer enjoy privileged access to investment-relevant information. Moreover, strict accounting, disclosure and auditing rules are often enforced by penalties which punish large and active investors. For example, under these strict conditions major shareholders can be held liable for the acts of their corporation and may be prosecuted under class action suits. Consequently,

12

strict accounting, disclosure and auditing rules discourage investors to acquire large stakes in a corporation and play an active role in corporate governance.

Without sustained information asymmetries between corporate insiders and outsiders, large investors can hardly benefit from holding an undiversified portfolio. Nondiversification costs cannot be recovered by information or governance advantages. As a result, large investors will be reluctant to forego risk diversification.

Reduced information asymmetries and low governance costs will encourage large numbers of investors to participate in capital market transactions. Regular disclosure of accurate investment-relevant information reduces investment uncertainty and makes capital market investments by corporate outsiders more calculable. Low information costs enable small investors to invest in corporate governance.

Weak accounting, disclosure and auditing laws, on the other hand, result in substantial information asymmetries between corporate insiders and outside investors. Small investors do not receive timely information concerning investment-relevant facts. Accounting options increase the costs of information interpretation. Outsiders must possess advanced accounting skills and have to invest considerable amounts of time in order to accurately assess a corporation's financial performance and economic perspective. In short, small investors are confronted with prohibitively high information costs which outweigh potential benefits from corporate governance.

Under weak accounting, disclosure and auditing rules, corporate insiders do not have to share their investment-relevant knowledge with outside investors. Hence large investors possess strong incentives to acquire majority stakes and invest in corporate governance. The resulting information advantages outweigh the costs of holding an undiversified portfolio. In addition, major shareholders do not have to fear liability charges in connection with disclosure policies.

Substantial informational asymmetries between corporate insiders and outsiders will discourage small investors to participate in capital market transactions. Weak accounting, disclosure and auditing regulations confront small investors with high levels of investment uncertainty and incalculable investment risk. High information barriers preclude small investors from corporate governance.

Regulation of insider trading

Insider regulation determines to what extent non-insiders are protected against insider trading. Strict laws against insider trading warrant criminal sanctions, including imprisonment for those who intentionally trade on the basis of unpublished material event information, and require corporate insiders such as directors, executives and major shareholders to disclose their security holdings and report all security transactions. Strict insider regulations reduce the incentive to engage in corporate governance, discourage ownership concentration, lead to an increase in the number of capital market participants, and encourage small investors to trade more frequently. Weak insider regulations rely on voluntary self-restraint and do not warrant criminal sanctions in case of non-compliance. Weak insider regulations promote corporate governance, encourage ownership concentration and discourage small investors from participating in capital market transactions.

Strict laws against insider trading reduce the incentive to invest into corporate governance. Active investors cannot recover governance costs by trading on the basis of insider knowledge acquired in the process of corporate governance. Without potential insider profits, investments into corporate governance become less attractive. Consequently, investors will be less willing to engage in corporate governance. Corporate managers will enjoy a rather wide range of discretionary freedom.

Strict insider regulations increase the costs of ownership concentration. Large and active investors cannot recover nondiversification costs through insider profits. Instead, strict insider regulations impose additional costs on major shareholders by requiring them to disclose security ownership and report security transactions. Major shareholders consistently risk being accused of insider trading when buying or selling prior to the disclosure of investment-relevant information. This practically precludes major shareholders from trading prior to dividend or profit reports. These additional costs favor risk diversification over ownership concentration (Bhide 1993: 36–7).

Strict insider regulations reduce the risk for small investors in trading with better informed market participants. Consequently, trading profits become more likely. Under these conditions, not only will the number of small investors who participate in capital market transactions increase, but small investors will also be encouraged to trade more frequently.

14

Weak insider regulations, on the other hand, promote corporate governance. Active investors are not effectively precluded from recovering governance costs by trading on the basis of insider knowledge acquired in the process of corporate governance. As a result, investments into corporate governance become more attractive. Governance activities will increase. Corporate managers will be closely monitored.

Weak laws against insider regulation reduce the costs of ownership concentration. Major investors do not have to disclose security ownership and report security transactions, nor do they have to restrict themselves from trading prior to dividend or profit reports. On the contrary, potential insider profits compensate major shareholders for foregoing risk diversification. Under these conditions, large investors possess strong incentives to hold undiversified portfolios.

Under weak insider regulations, small investors are exposed to the risk of trading with better informed market participants. In order to reduce this risk, they will either refrain from capital market participation or pursue long-term investment strategies. In the first case, the number of outside investors will decrease. In the second case, outside investors will trade less frequently.

Regulation of market manipulation

Capital market manipulations include all activities which are undertaken for the purpose of creating false or misleading capital market signals. The broad spectrum of capital market manipulations includes wash sales, matched orders, stop loss orders, short sales, and false or misleading transaction statements. Effective laws against capital market manipulation improve the informational accuracy of security prices. The resulting confidence in capital market signals encourages more investors to engage in capital market transactions. Ineffective prohibition of capital market manipulation, on the other hand, reduces the accuracy of price signals. As a result, potential investors will lose confidence in the price mechanism and will refrain from capital market participation.

(Anti-) takeover regulation

Attempts to regulate the market for corporate control may be divided into takeover and anti-takeover regulation. Takeover regulation

15

strengthens the rights of small shareholders in tender offers. So-called "best price rules" protect small shareholders against price discrimination. If a bidder subsequently increases the bid in an effort to induce more shareholders to tender their shares, the new offer will automatically become effective for all shares which have been tendered at the conditions of the initial bid. In addition, takeover laws may impose disclosure obligations on potential bidders, establish waiting periods during which offers have to remain open, require bidders to refrain from buying shares in the market during the bidding period, demand that bidders accept tendered shares in an oversubscribed partial offer on a pro rata rather than on a first-come-first-served basis, and grant withdrawal rights to target shareholders.

By depriving bidders of strategies that would facilitate acquisitions, takeover regulation shifts a portion of the potential takeover gains from bidders to target shareholders. This redistribution of takeover gains results in reduced takeover activities and leads to higher premiums in the case of successful offers.

While target shareholders benefit from tender offers, target managers lose their corporate-specific human capital when being replaced during hostile takeovers. The fear of losing corporate-specific human capital urges corporate managers to take preventive measures against hostile takeovers. The most effective measure would be to maximize shareholder wealth. If incumbent management succeeds in using corporate resources efficiently, there will be no reason for installing new managers after a successful takeover bid. Moreover, high share prices will prevent corporate raiders from submitting tender offers in the first place.

While maximizing shareholder wealth is the socially most beneficial measure against hostile takeovers, it is by no means the easiest way to ward off corporate raiders. It requires self-discipline and specialized management skills. Given these circumstances, it is not surprising that mediocre managers tend to prefer less demanding anti-takeover measures. The list of less demanding alternatives to maximizing shareholder wealth includes shark repellents, poison pills, greenmail, lock-up options, golden parachutes and litigation.

Shark repellents are corporate charter amendments which increase the stringency of takeover conditions. Popular anti-takeover amendments include super-majority provisions, dual- or multiple-class recapitalizations, staggered board elections, and voting right limitations. A typical poison pill is a special class of preferred stock which is issued to shareholders and which may be redeemed for cash in case of a change in corporate control. Greenmail refers to a transaction in which the target corporation repurchases a block of its common stock from an individual holder (e.g. the bidder), usually at a premium. Lock-up options entitle management to sell corporate assets at a discount in reaction to a tender offer. Golden parachutes trigger compensation payments to executives who are fired or demoted within a prespecified period of time following a change in corporate control. Depending upon the legal environment, litigation based on charges of securities fraud, anti-trust violations or violations against (anti-) takeover regulations may be an effective way to delay takeovers, increase takeover costs, and ultimately fight off hostile takeover bids.

Anti-takeover laws may restrict or prohibit anti-takeover measures, allocate the right to approve anti-takeover devices to shareholders, or grant target management wide discretion in anti-takeover defenses. Restriction or prohibition of anti-takeover measures facilitates corporate takeovers. Consequently, corporate screening becomes more profitable and thus more common. Frequent screening activities by corporate raiders who search for inefficiently managed corporations will reduce the agency costs of delegated management. On the other hand, managers will demand higher risk premiums as compensation for potential losses of corporate-specific human capital.

The right to approve anti-takeover measures would enable shareholders to install anti-takeover devices on the basis of a cost-benefit analysis. Whenever shareholders expect that the benefits, consisting primarily of an enhanced ability to bargain for higher takeover premiums and of lower risk premiums in executive compensation plans, outweigh the resulting increase in agency costs of delegated management, an anti-takeover device will be approved. Otherwise, it will not be approved.

Granting management unrestricted discretion in anti-takeover defenses would eventually dry out the market for corporate control.[5] Shareholders of public corporations would have to bear high agency costs, and corporate raiders would be either unwilling or unable to correct inefficient capital allocation and to improve corporate governance. Restricting management's discretion in anti-takeover defenses, on the other hand, would result in lower agency costs and would both motivate and enable corporate raiders to correct existing inefficiencies.

17

Diversification requirements

Diversification requirements force institutional investors and financial intermediaries to fragment their investment portfolios. Popular diversification requirements include provisions for investment companies, investment trusts, banks, pension funds and insurance companies to invest no more than a certain percentage (e.g. 5 percent) of their assets into a single company or hold no more than a certain percentage (e.g. 10 percent) of a single corporation's outstanding stock. These diversification requirements are commonly enforced by legal sanctions or tax penalties. Strict diversification requirements promote ownership fragmentation, enhance capital market liquidity[6] and discourage corporate governance by institutional investors and financial intermediaries (Bhide 1993: 39–40; Roe 1990: 12–15). Weak diversification requirements facilitate ownership concentration, reduce capital market liquidity and encourage corporate governance by institutional investors and financial intermediaries.

Institutional investors and financial intermediaries are able to accumulate larger amounts of funds than private investors. Consequently, they are in a privileged position to acquire large equity stakes and exercise substantial control over listed corporations. Strict diversification requirements preclude institutional investors and financial intermediaries from holding undiversified portfolios. As a result, corporate ownership becomes fragmented.

Institutional investors and financial intermediaries who are precluded from acquiring major equity stakes cannot exercise substantial corporate control, and possess little incentive to invest in corporate-specific knowledge. Without control opportunities and corporate-specific knowledge, institutional investors and financial intermediaries cannot earn an ongoing stream of information rents by holding on to their investments. Under these conditions, institutional investors and financial intermediaries will increase the turnover ratio of their portfolios. As they trade more frequently, capital market liquidity increases significantly.

Ownership fragmentation leads to weak governance structures. Institutional investors and financial intermediaries who own small fractions of a corporation's outstanding capital possess little incentive to invest in corporate governance. If they invested in corporate governance, they would have to incur all governance costs, whereas governance benefits would be shared by many investors. Diversified portfolios preclude them from internalizing large shares of the benefits which accrue from governance activities.

Without diversification requirements, institutional investors and financial intermediaries can acquire major equity stakes and exercise substantial corporate control. The nondiversification costs which result from ownership concentration may be recovered in the form of information rents. Concentrated ownership rights enable them to earn information rents by investing into corporate-specific knowledge. Under these circumstances, they possess strong incentives to acquire concentrated ownership rights and forego risk diversification.

Control benefits and information rents induce institutional investors and financial intermediaries who own concentrated ownership rights to hold on to their portfolios. High turnover ratios would sacrifice these control benefits and information rents. As they trade less frequently, capital market liquidity decreases significantly.

Ownership concentration leads to strong governance structures. Institutional investors and financial intermediaries who own large portions of a corporation's outstanding capital are able to internalize large amounts of the benefits which accrue from governance activities. Consequently, they possess strong incentives to invest into corporate governance.

Restriction of universal banking

The term "universal bank" usually refers to banks which provide the entire range of commercial and investment banking services (e.g. Schneider *et al.* 1978). Krümmel (1980: 35), however, suggests use of this term only when referring to banks which provide credit, deposit and underwriting services, and at the same time possess the potential of influencing non-banks through equity holdings, proxy rights and board membership.[7] To avoid confusion throughout this book, the first kind of universal bank will be called ordinary and the second kind privileged. When both kinds of universal banks are referred to neither term will be used.

Restriction of universal banking can be divided into a strong and a weak form. In its strong form, restriction of universal banking strictly separates the businesses of commercial and investment banking. Deposit-taking institutions are barred from exercising control over non-banks through equity ownership, proxy voting or board representation, and are precluded from issuing, underwriting, selling or distributing corporate securities, either directly or through affiliates. In its weak form, prohibition of universal banking allows banks to enter the business of commercial as well as investment banking, but precludes them from exercising control over non-banks through equity ownership, proxy voting and board representation. Consequently, the strong form prohibits all kinds of universal banks, whereas the weak form prohibits only privileged universal banks.

Weak form

Prohibiting banks from exerting control over non-banks through equity holding, proxy voting and board representation increases the costs of bank loans, enhances the problem of credit rationing, causes banks to withdraw long-term financial commitments, results in higher costs of financial distress for non-banks, activates the market for corporate control and cuts off important knowledge links.

Depriving universal banks of non-default control rights exposes their business loans to additional hazards. Without non-default control rights, banks are obliged to invest additional amounts into company screening, bond covenant design and loan monitoring in their effort to limit default risk. Generally, banks will try to pass the resulting cost increase on to their customers in the form of higher interest rates.

Despite additional investments into company screening, bond covenant design and loan monitoring, banks which have been deprived of non-default decision rights may fail to effectively limit default risk. Unlike additional governance costs, additional default risk cannot be compensated by higher interest rates. Accordingly, prohibition of privileged universal banks enhances the problem of credit rationing.

Barring banks from acquiring equity stakes in firms to which they lend will cause banks to withdraw long-term financial commitments. Banks which are precluded from acquiring equity stakes in non-banks have to bear the entire default risk of providing long-term capital for investments into the distant future (e.g. research and development expenditures) without being able to benefit from abnormal investment returns. While allowing banks to acquire equity stocks in firms to which they provide long-term debt would ease this asymmetry, prohibition of equity ownership by banks forces non-banks to rely exclusively on equity-funding for long-term investment projects.

Non-default control rights enable privileged universal banks to take precautionary actions at an early stage of a customer's financial distress. Unless the bank expects the firm's assets to be more valuable under bankruptcy procedures than as a going concern, corporate restructuring will be preferred over entering bankruptcy procedures. However, prohibition of equity holdings, proxy voting and board representation prevents universal banks from initiating corporate restructuring via non-default control rights. Instead of helping viable firms to escape bankruptcy procedures, banks which are deprived of non-default control rights over non-banks are more likely to force a financially troubled firm into bankruptcy in order to acquire decision rights over the firm's remaining assets. Providing a financially distressed firm with additional funds to facilitate reorganization and restructuring exposes a bank which does not possess non-default decision rights to uncontrollable hazards.

Universal banks which exert non-default control over non-banks have both the incentive and opportunity to fight off hostile takeover attempts in the industry sector. A bank which provides non-banks with business loans acquires firm-specific information during its screening and monitoring activities. This information enables the bank to gain continuous information rents as long as the underlying lending relationship is kept alive. Hostile takeovers threaten to terminate these lending relationships. In an effort to protect their information rents, banks will attempt to resist such takeovers. Equity holdings, proxy voting rights and board representation provide privileged universal banks with the necessary authority to succeed in fighting off corporate raiders.

Even if information rents were not at stake, privileged universal banks might still prefer to resist takeover attempts and initiate bank-guided corporate restructurings. By initiating corporate restructurings, privileged universal banks are able to harvest at least part of the restructuring benefits which would otherwise accrue to corporate raiders.

Without equity holdings, proxy voting rights and board representation, universal banks can neither successfully fight off corporate raiders nor effectively initiate corporate restructurings. In the absence of privileged universal banks, corporate raiders can expect positive returns from screening target firms and submitting tender offers. An active market for corporate control will be the logical result. Accordingly, the burden of disciplining management teams of public

21

corporations will shift from privileged universal banks to capital market forces.

Finally, prohibiting banks from holding equity stocks in non-banks, exerting proxy voting rights and nominating board representatives will cut off crucial knowledge links.[8] Non-default control rights enable privileged universal banks to create a network of personal relationships between bank executives and industry leaders. This network provides an important communication channel. Bank executives who meet regularly with industry leaders and who are personally involved in corporate decision making acquire more than valuable explicit information about current economic facts and future developments. They are in a unique position for generating important tacit knowledge with regard to managers, corporations and industries. Prohibition of privileged universal banks destroys these networks as well as the related communication advantages.

Strong form

In its strong form, prohibition of universal banking separates commercial and investment banking. Unrestricted universal banking will undermine the role of equity and debt markets in providing corporate capital. Information economies of scope allow ordinary universal banks to provide investment services at lower cost than investment banks. As a result, investment banks cannot effectively compete with ordinary universal banks. Without the competition of investment banks, however, universal banks will focus their efforts primarily on the lending business, which, given that most loans will regularly be prolonged, generates an ongoing stream of information rents compared to one-time profits in the investment business. The attempt by universal banks to promote their commercial business at the expense of investment activities will finally lead to an erosion of capital markets.[9]

Separation of commercial and investment banking, on the other hand, enhances the competitiveness of investment banks by preventing commercial banks from realizing information economies of scope in the investment business. In the absence of competition from universal banks, investment banks will not only be able to survive, but will also contribute to capital market efficiency. Investment banking, unlike universal banking, is not primarily information-driven, but rather innovation-driven. Financial innovation is the major source of profit increases in the investment business. Accordingly, active investment banks are the essence of advanced capital markets.

Conclusion: neoclassical versus relational regulation

The spectrum of alternative regulatory environments is rather wide. Neoclassical and relational regulation may be identified as the extreme poles at each end of this wide spectrum. Table 1.1 summarizes the distinguishing characteristics of neoclassical and relational regulation.

Table 1.1 Distinguishing features of neoclassical and relational regulation

	Neoclassical regulation	*Relational regulation*
Theoretical foundation	Neoclassical economics	Property rights theory, agency theory, economics of governance
Focus	Allocative efficiency	Coordinative efficiency
Objective	Elimination of capital market imperfections	Enhancement of corporate governance and reduction of the costs of financial distress
Accounting, disclosure and auditing regulation	Strict (extensive, well-specified, and well-enforced)	Weak/vague
Insider regulation	Strict laws against insider trading	No/weak laws against insider trading
Regulation of market manipulation	Effectively prohibited	No/weak prohibition
(Anti-)Takeover regulation	Anti-takeover oriented	Takeover oriented
Diversification requirements	Yes	No
Restriction of universal banking	Prohibition of universal banking (strong form)	No prohibition of universal banking
Resulting investment perspective	Short-term	Long-term

Neoclassical regulation is based on the theoretical foundations of neoclassical economics (e.g. Debreu 1959; Arrow and Hahn 1971). According to neoclassical economics, all markets which are perfectly competitive efficiently allocate scarce resources (see for example Kreps 1990: 263–98). Within perfectly competitive capital markets, firms will issue securities at a price which, first, equals the value of the (expected) marginal product of capital; second, equals the (expected) marginal investment utility for each investor; and third, clears markets. However, most of the neoclassical assumptions, such as completely informed market participants, unmanipulated market prices, and price-taking behavior, do not hold in the real world. Most markets are subject to major imperfections. Consequently, neoclassical regulation is driven by the objective to eliminate existing market imperfections as far as possible.

In the case of capital markets, neoclassical regulation aims to reduce the information asymmetries among market participants by installing extensive, well-specified and well-enforced accounting, disclosure and auditing rules. Prohibition of insider trading is intended to neutralize the remaining information asymmetries. Strict laws against market manipulation guarantee fair transactions. Diversification requirements, anti-takeover laws and prohibition of universal banking further enforce the neoclassical ideal of perfectly competitive markets by preventing capital market participants from acquiring market power. Although neoclassical regulators are aware that the neoclassical ideal of perfectly competitive markets remains a utopian vision in the real world, their intention is to enhance capital market efficiency by eliminating at least some of the existing market imperfections.

While neoclassical regulation focuses primarily on allocative efficiency, relational regulation concentrates on governance efficiency. The theoretical foundations of relational regulation are provided primarily by the property rights literature (e.g. Picot 1981; Demsetz and Lehn 1985; Shleifer and Vishny 1986), agency theory (e.g. Jensen and Meckling 1976; Bhide 1993), and the economics of governance (e.g. Williamson 1996). Within the framework of these theories, capital market imperfections such as ownership concentration, market manipulation or insider trading, are scrutinized with regard to their effect on corporate governance. From a relational perspective, most of the neoclassical market imperfections are not considered harmful, but are perceived as a means to economize on governance costs. Attempts to concentrate corporate ownership rights, for example, are regarded as an efficient response to the governance deficiencies within publicly held corporations. Ownership fragmentation and the resulting attenuation of property rights discourage market participants to invest in corporate governance. If property rights are attenuated, active investors will have to bear the full governance costs while large parts of the governance benefits will accrue to others (mainly passive investors). Under these conditions, investments into corporate governance do not yield positive returns. Concentrated ownership rights correct these disincentives by enabling active investors to internalize substantial parts of the resulting governance benefits.

In order to acquire concentrated ownership rights, active investors will have to forego the benefits of risk diversification. Unless compensated otherwise, high opportunity costs will force potentially active investors to refrain from holding undiversified investment portfolios and engage in corporate governance. Since all capital market participants will benefit from the governance activities of active investors, a regulatory environment which consists of weak accounting, disclosure and auditing rules and does not effectively restrict insider trading and market manipulation may be regarded as the result of a unanimous effort to enhance corporate governance by compensating active investors for the opportunity costs of holding undiversified portfolios.[10] Ownership concentration and corporate governance are further facilitated by takeover-oriented regulations and by the absence of diversification requirements.

The most important element of relational regulation is the promotion of privileged universal banking. Within a relational regulatory environment, deposit-taking institutions are encouraged to engage in investment banking activities and are entitled to exercise non-default decision rights over non-banks through equity holdings, proxy voting and board representation. These rights not only enable banks to realize economies of scope, but, more importantly, allow them to govern their business loans through a combination of debt and equity control rights. The resulting governance structure at least partly eliminates the problem of credit rationing. It further facilitates the provision of bank loans for long-term investment projects and reduces the costs of financial distress. While commercial banks and ordinary universal banks rely on bankruptcy procedures to acquire decision rights over a customer's assets, privileged universal banks can initiate corporate restructuring at an early stage of financial stress.

Since investments into corporate governance are usually highly specific, investors who do not possess additional safeguards to protect these governance investments will be exposed to uncontrollable risk. To the extent that these investors act rationally, they will refrain from investing into corporate-specific knowledge. Weak governance structures will be the unavoidable consequence. Ownership concentration and privileged universal banking, on the other hand, provide the necessary safeguards to protect specific investments into corporate governance. As a result, privileged universal banks as well as active private investors, institutional investors and financial intermediaries who possess concentrated ownership rights will earn a continuous stream of governance rents. The prospect of protected governance rents will induce privileged universal banks, active private investors, institutional investors and financial intermediaries to engage in long-term investment relations.

Contrary to relational regulation, neoclassical regulation eliminates the prospect of protected governance rents. Consequently, neoclassical investors are less likely to commit themselves to long-term investment relations, and will therefore discount expected future cash flows at a higher rate than active investors under relational regulation.

This dichotomization of regulatory environments represents an extreme simplification. It has been introduced in order to reduce the underlying empirical complexity. Neoclassical and relational regulation are by no means the only forms of regulatory environments. They represent the opposite poles of a wide regulatory spectrum.

ORGANIZATIONAL MODES OF CAPITAL ALLOCATION AND CORPORATE GOVERNANCE

In this section, unintermediated capital markets, investment companies and investment trusts, banks, holding companies, multi-divisionalized firms, leveraged buyout associations and financial keiretsu will be introduced as alternative modes of capital allocation and corporate governance. After introducing its basic features, each organizational mode will be analyzed with respect to the kind and amount of knowledge it is able to generate and utilize during the process of capital allocation, the attained level of risk diversification and the prevailing agency problems. The respective knowledge analysis will be based on the information and knowledge taxonomy developed in the following paragraphs. Risk diversification will be assessed in accordance with the principles of portfolio selection. Agency theory will be employed to identify the agency costs associated with each organizational mode.

Information and knowledge taxonomy Allocating capital to high-yield uses requires two kinds of information: event information and effect information.[11] Event information transmits knowledge about actions, incidents, or circumstances which may have a significant impact on investment risk and return. For example, the discovery of previously unknown oil wells, the development of new products, interest rate changes, takeover bids, privatization plans and indicators of shifts within consumer preferences are potential contents of event information. As these examples show, event information may either refer to past facts or indicate future possibilities.

Event information does not include information about the impact of its content on investment risk and return. Event information has to be translated into economic effects and their impact on investment risk and return. This translation process relies on effect information. Effect information is based on knowledge about causative economic relationships. This kind of knowledge may be based on theories, experience or pure intuition. It is usually incorporated in the form of if-then clauses (e.g. if a corporation receives a takeover bid, then share prices of this corporation will rise). Pieces of effect information are often aggregated into complex effect chains. Information aggregation allows investors to use large amounts of effect information despite the limits of human information processing.[12]

Using effect information, event information may be categorized according to its degree of specificity. Event information is labeled as unspecific or general, if the underlying action, incident or circumstance (e.g. increasing inflation) affects the returns of many securities. Event information is classified as semi-specific if the underlying fact (e.g. new import restrictions on foreign cars) causes price changes within a certain group of financial securities. Finally, event information is regarded as highly specific if the underlying fact (e.g. a takeover bid) causes a price change in only one financial security.

The private value of event information usually increases with its degree of specialization. An event information which indicates that the market price of one security will change by 10 percent is of higher value to an investor whose financial resources are limited than an event information which indicates that the prices of ten securities will each change by 1 percent. Keep in mind that the social values of both kinds of information are equal.

Event information may further be classified on the basis of information accessibility and information completeness. Costless access to an information source by all members of society results in public information. Private information, on the other hand, is based on privileged access to relevant information sources. An information event is complete if it contains all relevant facts concerning the underlying event. It is incomplete if it contains only partial indications concerning the underlying event. As Figure 1.2 shows, the different types of information which result from the combination of both dimensions generate four (five) categories of knowledge.

Public and complete event information creates common knowledge. Consider, for instance, a publicly announced takeover bid. Public and incomplete event information will result in fragmentary

	Complete information	Incomplete information
Public Information	Common knowledge	Fragmented (common) knowledge
Private Information	Insider knowledge	Fragmented (insider) knowledge Scattered knowledge

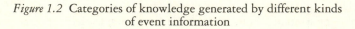

Figure 1.2 Categories of knowledge generated by different kinds of event information

28

common knowledge. Government officials who publicly stress the problem of deficit spending without clarifying how they want to solve it create fragmentary common knowledge.

Private and complete event information leads to insider knowledge. Board members, for example, frequently possess insider knowledge about corporate-specific events, such as takeover bids or quarterly earnings, until they are publicly announced. Fragmentary insider knowledge is created by incomplete private event information. Although CEOs and divisional managers are usually well informed about corporate and division earnings, they often possess only fragmentary insider knowledge about the current cost structure of single products. A special kind of fragmentary insider knowledge is scattered knowledge. This kind of knowledge is generated whenever a complete set of event information is broken up into many incomplete parts and dispersed as private information throughout society. If accumulated, these individual parts would form a complete information set. However, limited access to each information source prohibits investors from accumulating scattered knowledge. The classification which has been introduced in this section refers to idealized types of information and knowledge; empirical differences are rather by degree than by kind.

Unintermediated capital markets

This analysis of unintermediated capital markets is divided into three parts, describing the general characteristics of unintermediated capital markets; the specific features of capital markets under neoclassical regulation; and the specific features of capital markets under relational regulation.

General characteristics of unintermediated capital markets

Capital markets can be divided into debt and equity markets. The general characteristics of capital allocation and corporate governance within debt markets are analyzed in the first subsection. The second subsection deals with the general aspects of capital allocation and corporate governance within equity markets. Conclusions are offered in the third subsection.

Debt markets

The institution of debt is defined by the following contingent rights and obligations. Debt guarantees a fixed return to its suppliers in states when the borrowing firm is not bankrupt. In states of bankruptcy, the suppliers of debt will receive the right to decide about the future operations of the firm and will be entitled to claim a proportion of the firm's remaining funds. This proportion will be determined by seniority rights and the amount of debt invested by each claimant. Although debt does not entitle its suppliers to exercise non-default decision rights, debt reduces the agency costs of free cash flow (Jensen 1986). Even entrenched managers cannot withhold interest and principal payments without risking bankruptcy procedures. Debt is originally issued in primary debt markets and subsequently traded in secondary debt markets.

Primary debt markets Within perfect markets,[13] prices equal supply and demand and allocate scarce resources to their highest yield uses. Furthermore, price changes rapidly adjust economic activities to new circumstances (Hayek 1945). In short, the price mechanism of perfect markets is a marvel. However, real markets do not fulfill the textbook conditions of perfect markets. Primary debt markets are no exception.

The price of debt is specified by interest rates. Information and incentive asymmetries prevent interest rates from perfectly adjusting to changes in supply and demand. Information asymmetries arise if potential borrowers cannot effectively signal their risk-preferences. Under these circumstances, creditors cannot assess the default risk of their loans and do not know whether borrowers will react to higher interest rates by undertaking riskier investments.

Incentive asymmetries are caused by limited liability. Under limited liability, corporate owners are indifferent with respect to all possible states of bankruptcy. The losses which they will incur in case of bankruptcy are limited to the amount of equity which they have invested, regardless of their corporation's outstanding liabilities. In states of solvency, on the other hand, corporate owners will benefit from increasing corporate value. As residual claimants, corporate owners will try to maximize the expected return of all corporate investment projects (assuming they are risk-neutral).

Creditors, on the other hand, will be indifferent with respect to all possible states of solvency. Regardless of the corporation's market value, creditors cannot earn more than the fixed payments they are entitled to by the debt contract. In case of bankruptcy, however, creditors will receive decision rights and will be entitled to claim ownership of the firm's remaining funds. Consequently, creditors will benefit from increasing corporate value in case of bankruptcy. As claimants of fixed payments and holders of contingent decision rights, creditors will try to minimize the risk of losing their capital.[14] The financial benefits and losses which will accrue to corporate owners and creditors under different states of bankruptcy and solvency are shown in Figure 1.3.

The incentive and information asymmetries between corporate owners and creditors will lead to credit rationing. As Stiglitz and Weiss[15] have shown, an increase in interest rates will induce borrowers who are not risk-averse to undertake riskier projects, if the interest rate increase reduces the expected return from a project with a lower probability of bankruptcy by more than it reduces the expected return from a project with a higher probability of bankruptcy. Borrowers who are risk-averse, on the other hand, will reduce their demand for debt if increasing interest rates result in a higher probability of bankruptcy. As a result, the overall default risk within primary debt markets is likely to increase in response to higher interest rates. Creditors who do not possess accurate information about the risk-preferences of potential borrowers and cannot exercise control over the borrowing company's investment decisions

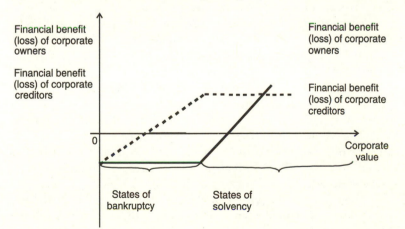

Figure 1.3 Financial benefits (losses) of corporate owners and creditors under limited liablility

will be exposed to higher default risk if they decide to remain in the market. Being aware of these consequences, rational creditors who have neither *ex ante* information about their borrowers' risk preferences nor *ex post* control opportunities over a borrower's investment decisions will prefer to withhold credits. Consequently, borrowers will be confronted with credit rationing as primary debt markets fail to equal credit supply and demand via interest rate changes.

The information and incentive asymmetries which lead to credit rationing may be reduced through reputational effects, collateral, equity and protective covenants. Reputation serves both as a signal and as a hostage. As a signal, it informs potential lenders that a borrower has lived up to past promises. Once acquired, reputation is a valuable economic resource. It enables borrowers to escape credit rationing. Since lenders may ruin a borrower's reputation in case of default, reputation serves as a hostage. However, reputation will serve as an effective hostage only if the costs incurred through loss of reputation outweigh the expected benefits from acting against the lender's interest. For example, reputation is an ineffective hostage if a borrower is lending capital for the last time. The economic value of reputation will be zero in this case.

The most effective device to reduce information and incentive asymmetries between borrowers and lenders is collateral securities.[16] Collateral entitles lenders to claim ownership rights on certain assets in case of default. Hence the remaining default risk is limited by the liquidation value of these assets. Lenders will prefer unspecific assets as collateral because these assets do not lose much value when liquidated. Specific assets on the other hand will lose most if not all of their value when liquidated.[17]

Equity can reduce the information and incentive asymmetries between borrowers and creditors in two different ways. First, low debt-equity ratios serve as a cushion against bankruptcy and represent a credible commitment to prevent default. The larger the amount of equity in relation to debt, the smaller are the chances of bankruptcy and the stronger is the borrower's commitment to prevent default. Second, equity ownership provides creditors with an opportunity to acquire non-default decision rights. Creditors who possess equity stakes are able to control the default risk of their loans, and so will lend at more favorable terms than creditors who are precluded from exercising non-default decision rights

Besides reputation, collateral securities and equity, protective covenants written into the debt contract are a common means of reducing default risk. These covenants can be divided into four categories:

1 covenants which restrict the issuance of new debt
2 covenants which restrict dividend payments to stockholders
3 covenants which restrict merger activities
4 covenants which restrict disposition over the company's assets.[18]

Although reputation, collateral, equity and bond covenants may enable an established company to escape credit rationing, they are of little help for an unestablished company. Start-up firms do not have a reputation, usually do not own many unspecific assets and are short on equity. Due to the price imperfections within primary debt markets, unestablished firms cannot finance their innovative activities by issuing bonds, even if they expect high returns and promise to pay higher interest rates than other borrowers. As a consequence, debt is not automatically allocated to its highest-yield uses by the price mechanism. As the breakdown of the US junk bond market has revealed, the price mechanism cannot solve the information and incentive problems which prevail within primary debt markets.[19]

Secondary debt markets   Secondary debt markets enhance credit liquidity by enabling lenders to sell their claims before maturity. However, secondary debt markets suffer from even larger information asymmetries than primary debt markets. Potential buyers do not know *ex ante* whether creditors are offering their claims for liquidity reasons or in reaction to increasing default risk. These information asymmetries will lead to a market breakdown unless liquidity traders can effectively signal their true intentions.
    An effective signal must fulfill the following requirements:

1 the benefits of signaling the true intentions must exceed the costs of producing the signal, and
2 the benefits of signaling false intentions must be lower than the costs of producing false signals.

Given these preconditions, only true liquidity traders will have an incentive to produce effective signals.[20] Since there is no signal available to liquidity traders which fulfills these requirements, secondary markets for risky credits will break down. Secondary debt markets can only be established for low-risk (almost riskless) bonds.

Equity markets

Equity holders possess non-default decision rights and are entitled to claim a proportionate share of the residual income. Equity rights are originally sold in primary equity markets in exchange for the provision of capital and are subsequently traded in secondary equity markets.

Primary equity markets Primary equity markets allocate capital through (1) initial public offerings, and (2) seasoned public offerings.

(1) The amount of debt which can be raised by a firm is usually limited in various ways (amount of equity, reputation, specificity of assets). As long as a firm's legal form requires personal identity of ownership and control, the amount of equity which can be raised is limited as well. Privately held companies which need large amounts of capital to finance their activities have to transform into publicly held corporations in order to raise the necessary amounts of capital. Transformation into a publicly held corporation requires that equity rights are offered to a large number of investors. The price mechanism will allocate these equity rights into the hands of those investors who are willing to pay the highest price, i.e. who are willing to provide the largest amounts of equity capital in exchange for equity rights.

Unlike equity rights, equity capital is allocated on the basis of individual expectations. There is no price mechanism within primary equity markets which allocates equity capital. Investors will provide equity capital to those corporations which are expected to generate the highest returns. These expectations may be based on the knowledge aggregated and transmitted by the price mechanism within secondary equity markets.

The market for initial public offerings suffers from substantial information asymmetries between issuers and investors. Issuers, e.g. company founders and managers, have an information advantage over investors. Insider knowledge enables them to assess the value of the offered equity rights much more accurately than outside investors not having access to insider knowledge.

Corporate equity rights may be offered in order to realize profitable investments or in order to benefit from information asymmetries. Outsiders always have to fear the latter. Rational owners who expect high returns from their company's investments will prefer to finance new investments by issuing additional debt in an effort to profit from leverage effects. However, credit rationing may preclude them from issuing additional debt. In this case, going public is the only way to raise enough capital in order to realize new investment projects.

Non-owner managers, on the other hand, will promote initial public offerings in order to enlarge their discretionary freedom and to reduce the risk of bankruptcy. Ownership dispersion reduces the incentives of each individual shareholder to invest into corporate governance. In the case of bankruptcy, non-owner managers would not only lose their job, but would also incur large losses in human capital.

Outside investors do not know the true motive behind each initial public offering. They cannot determine whether a company is subjected to credit rationing, nor do they possess the necessary insider knowledge to accurately assess the market value of the offered equity rights.

The costs of reducing these information asymmetries are prohibitively high within unintermediated primary equity markets. Potential investors would have to gather information about the true motives behind an initial public offering and would have to acquire insider knowledge in order to accurately assess the market value of the offered equity rights. Given these difficulties, issuers who try to escape credit rationing by raising equity possess strong incentives to credibly signal their true motives as well as the accurate market value of the offered equity rights. However, unintermediated primary equity markets do not provide issuers with an opportunity to produce effective signals.

Reputation and guarantee would be effective signals. However, since going public is a unique event within the life cycle of each company, founders and managers cannot build up a reputation for honest initial public offerings.[21] Nor do they have the necessary capital to provide investors with credible guarantees. If they had the necessary capital, they would not have to raise equity capital through initial public offerings in order to realize new investment projects.

Unintermediated equity markets cannot effectively reduce the information asymmetries associated with initial public offerings. Issuers depend on the support of financial intermediaries such as investment banks. Financial intermediaries have the potential of providing credible guarantees and are able to acquire a reputation by repeatedly engaging in successful initial public offerings.

35

(2) Seasoned public offerings suffer from similar information asymmetries as do initial public offerings. Due to the lack of insider knowledge, potential investors neither know the true motive behind a seasoned public offering, nor are they able to accurately assess the market value of the offered equity rights. Consequently, potential investors do not know whether a seasoned public offering is motivated by credit rationing or opportunism. However, the information problems which are associated with seasoned public offerings can be solved within unintermediated equity markets.

Outstanding shares of the issuing corporation are already traded in secondary markets. The price of these outstanding shares transmits aggregated information about the expectations that market participants have developed about the corporation's future cash flow. Since potential investors have the opportunity to buy outstanding shares in secondary markets instead of signing newly issued shares in the primary market, the current market price of outstanding shares reflects the upper limit of the price which the corporation is able to demand in the primary market.

Empirical evidence reveals that a decrease (increase) in a corporation's debt-equity ratio leads to an increase (decline) in the corporation's share price.[22] Current owners suffer an immediate loss of wealth as soon as they decide to issue new equity (see Gale and Stiglitz 1989). This market response reduces the incentives to issue new equity for opportunistic reasons. Current owners who are aware of the market's reaction will approve seasoned public offerings only if they expect a subsequent increase in share prices which will offset the original loss. Consequently, the price mechanism of secondary markets has the potential to solve the problems which arise in relation to the information asymmetries associated with seasoned public offerings.

Secondary equity markets Although secondary equity markets do not allocate any capital from the savings to the industry sector, they do perform two major functions within the process of capital allocation and corporate governance: (1) secondary equity markets support primary capital markets, and (2) they reallocate corporate ownership rights.

(1) Secondary equity markets support primary capital markets in three ways. The ability of secondary equity markets to reduce the incentive and information asymmetries which are associated with seasoned public offerings has already been discussed. In addition,

secondary equity markets provide stockholders with instant liquidity and, more importantly, aggregate and transmit valuable information through the price mechanism.

The existence of secondary equity markets enables investors to meet unexpected liquidity demands by selling corporate stock. High levels of market liquidity ensure that corporate stock can be sold at current market prices. Consequently, savers do not have to keep large cash deposits, but can invest their savings in corporate stock without incurring high illiquidity costs.

The kind and amount of information which is aggregated and transmitted by secondary equity markets has been the focus of intensive discussions among capital market theorists. Fama's classification of informational efficiency has become a widely accepted basis for this discussion. Fama (1970: 383) distinguishes three forms of informational efficiency. Secondary equity markets are informationally efficient in a strong sense, if stock prices aggregate and convey all public and private knowledge. If stock prices aggregate and convey all public knowledge, secondary equity markets are informationally efficient in Fama's semi-strong sense. Secondary equity markets are informationally efficient in a weak sense, if current stock prices aggregate and convey all knowledge which has been aggregated and transmitted by historical stock prices.

As Grossman and Stiglitz (1976, 1980) have shown, capital markets can only be informationally efficient in a strong sense with respect to knowledge generated by costless information. If stock prices already convey all available knowledge, market participants cannot obtain positive returns from investing into information activities. Accordingly, information activities will be limited to the acquisition of costless information and stock prices will remain incompletely arbitraged with respect to knowledge based on costly information. Empirical evidence supports this argumentation. Lorie and Niederhoffer (1968), Jaffe (1974), Finnerty (1976) and Seyhun (1982) report that corporate insiders consistently outperform the market.[23] Consequently, stock prices are not perfectly arbitraged with respect to insider knowledge.

While secondary equity markets cannot be informationally efficient in a strong sense, they are at least informationally efficient in Fama's semi-strong sense. Since public knowledge is based on costless information, stock prices are fully arbitraged with respect to public knowledge. Market participants cannot outperform the market by trading solely on the basis of public knowledge. Empirical evidence could not refute the hypothesis that capital markets are informationally efficient in Fama's semi-strong sense (see Malkiel 1987; LeRoy 1989).

Informational efficiency in Fama's semi-strong sense includes informational efficiency in the weak sense. Historical prices are available to the public at no cost. If secondary equity markets are fully arbitraged with respect to public knowledge, investors cannot realize abnormal returns by trading on the basis of historical prices. Future price changes cannot be estimated on the basis of past price movements.[24]

While semi-strong informational efficiency implies that other information mechanisms cannot aggregate and transmit larger amounts of public knowledge than the price mechanism of secondary equity markets, information inefficiency in the strong sense does not imply that other information mechanisms aggregate and transmit larger amounts of private knowledge than secondary equity markets. Comparative organizational analysis has to be based on relative instead of absolute informational efficiency. An organizational mode is informationally efficient in a relative sense if there does not exist another organizational mode which aggregates and transmits larger amounts of knowledge. Since the amount of private knowledge which is aggregated and conveyed by unintermediated capital markets depends upon capital market regulations, the relative informational efficiency of unintermediated capital markets cannot be assessed in general.

(2) Another important function of secondary equity markets is the reallocation of equity rights. The price mechanism of secondary equity markets reallocates equity rights to those investors who are willing to pay the highest price. This reallocation process guarantees that those investors who are able to maximize corporate value have the opportunity to acquire corporate ownership. From this perspective, secondary equity markets serve as markets for corporate control.

Markets for corporate control not only reallocate ownership rights, they also force corporate executives to maximize shareholder wealth. Shareholders who are not satisfied with the performance of corporate executives may express their dissatisfaction in either of two ways: voice or exit.[25] Voice refers to the attempt to engage in corporate governance and dismiss corporate executives who fail to maximize shareholder wealth. Exit refers to the decision to sell corporate shares in response to poor corporate performance.

In case of ownership concentration, voice is an efficient mechanism to restrain managerial misbehavior. Major shareholders who decide to invest into corporate governance do not only have to bear the entire costs of their monitoring activities, they are also able to internalize sufficiently large parts of the resulting governance benefits (see Demsetz and Lehn 1985: 1156; Shleifer and Vishny 1986: 465–71; Zeckhauser and Pound 1990).

In case of ownership fragmentation, exit is the preferred response to corporate inefficiencies. Small shareholders who decide to invest in corporate governance will have to bear the entire costs of their governance activities, whereas the resulting governance benefits will have to be shared with many others. For small shareholders, voice is an economically unattractive option.

If a majority of unsatisfied shareholders chooses the exit option, corporate share prices will decline. As a consequence, raising new capital will become more difficult, and more importantly, corporate takeovers will become more likely. Low market capitalization signals corporate inefficiencies and potential takeover profits. Incumbent managers possess strong incentives to prevent corporate takeovers. A change in corporate control will not only cost them their job, but will also lead to substantial losses of corporate-specific human capital. As a result, an active market for corporate control reduces the governance inefficiencies which are caused by ownership fragmentation.

However, the market for corporate control suffers from several imperfections. Information uncertainties about potential takeover profits may lead to adverse selection (Akerlof 1970). If shareholders were well informed about corporate inefficiencies and potential takeover gains, their willingness to accept (reject) a takeover bid would indicate that the takeover bid is too high (low) (Stiglitz 1985: 137). Consequently, bidders would be in a no-win situation. In case of ownership concentration, this problem may result in a breakdown of the market for corporate control. Major shareholders usually possess accurate knowledge about corporate inefficiencies and potential takeover gains. Since corporate executives are closely monitored under ownership concentration, a potential breakdown of the market for corporate control does not impair corporate governance. In case of dispersed corporate ownership, on the other hand, the problem of adverse selection is unlikely to occur. Prohibitively high information costs will prevent small investors from acquiring accurate knowledge about corporate inefficiencies and potential takeover profits.

In case of ownership fragmentation, corporate raiders are likely to possess information advantages over shareholders. Corporate raiders invest in corporate screening in order to discover corporate inefficiencies and assess potential takeover profits. A takeover bid signals target shareholders that corporate raiders expect post-takeover increases in corporate value. Knowing that the success of the takeover bid does not depend upon the willingness of a single shareholder to accept the bid, small shareholders will try to benefit from post-takeover increases in corporate value by refusing to tender their shares. However, they will only succeed in free-riding on the restructuring activities provided by corporate raiders if a majority of shareholders accepts the offer. If a majority of shareholders tries to free-ride, the offer will fail and shareholders will remain empty-handed. Based on this argumentation, Grossman and Hart (1980) conclude that free-riding will cause a breakdown of the market for corporate control. From the small shareholder's perspective, it is always rational not to tender. If the takeover bid is successful, a small shareholder will benefit from corporate restructuring. If the offer fails, a small shareholder could not have changed the outcome by accepting the bid. However, empirical evidence does not support this conclusion. Small shareholders do not always refuse to tender.

According to Stiglitz (1975b), another imperfection of the market for corporate control results from the signaling effects of takeover bids. The original bidder unwillingly signals that the target corporation is undervalued. Other investors can enter the bidding without having to incur high discovery costs by screening a large number of corporations. If other bidders enter the bidding process, original bidders cannot expect positive returns from their investments into corporate screening. As a result, nobody will invest in the search for target corporations and takeover activity will cease. Empirical evidence does not support this theoretical conclusion. Low discovery costs may provide a reasonable explanation for the existence of active markets for corporate control. If share prices signal which corporations are attractive targets, the original bidder does not have to incur prohibitively high discovery costs by screening a large number of corporations.[26]

The described imperfections are unlikely to result in a breakdown of the market for corporate control. Anti-takeover measures and anti-takeover regulations present a much more dangerous threat to active markets for corporate control than unintended signaling effects or free-riding attempts.

Conclusion

The efficiency of unintermediated capital markets depends heavily upon the price signals and disciplinary effects of secondary equity markets. Allocative efficiency of unintermediated capital markets is determined by the kind and amount of knowledge which is aggregated and transmitted through the price mechanism of secondary equity markets. There is no price mechanism within primary equity markets which allocates scarce equity. Capital allocation within primary equity markets is based on expectations about future cash flows. The price mechanism of primary debt markets suffers from the effects of credit rationing. Secondary debt markets do not have an independent price mechanism. Prices in secondary debt markets are determined by the prevailing interest rate within primary debt markets. The inability of interest rates to perfectly adjust to changes in supply and demand precludes primary and secondary debt markets from aggregating and transmitting accurate investment relevant information. Participants of primary equity and debt markets rely on the information aggregated and transmitted by secondary equity markets.

Corporate governance within unintermediated capital markets is based on one of two mechanisms. In case of ownership concentration, major stockholders will invest in corporate governance. In case of ownership fragmentation, corporate governance depends primarily upon the disciplinary effects of secondary equity markets. Stockholders possess no economic incentive to invest into corporate governance. The governance effects of debt are limited to a reduction in the agency costs of free cash flow. The disciplinary mechanisms within primary equity markets rely on the assistance of price effects within secondary equity markets.

The prevailing governance mechanism, as well as the kind and amount of knowledge which is aggregated and conveyed by stock prices, is determined by the regulatory environment. Neoclassical capital markets rely on different governance mechanisms, and aggregate and transmit different kinds and amounts of knowledge than relational capital markets.

Neoclassical capital markets

Neoclassical capital market regulations reduce the information advantages of corporate insiders. Small investors enjoy a more level playing field. Thus neoclassical regulation encourages more members of society to participate in capital market transactions. As the number of investors who participate in capital market transactions increases, stock prices become more likely to aggregate and transmit large amounts of scattered knowledge.

Non-insiders will base their investment decisions primarily on public information and individual expectations. Unless these expectations differ among investors, only liquidity- and diversification-related transactions will occur. Two investors who have already diversified all unsystematic risk and who do not trade for liquidity reasons will exchange securities only on the basis of different individual expectations. Differing individual expectations are the result of incomplete private knowledge. In a society which is built on specialization and division of labor, almost every member i has privileged access to a different information source providing him or her with rather unique pieces of scattered knowledge Σ_i. If this particular person participates in capital market transactions, he or she will not only contribute Σ_i, but will also produce noise ε_i. This noise term reflects the ignorance of the respective market participant. If the ε_i are uncorrelated, the amount of noise incorporated by stock prices will decrease as the number of market participants increases. Under this condition, neoclassical capital markets are able to aggregate and transmit large amounts of scattered knowledge. If the ε_i are correlated, an increase in the number of capital market participants will magnify rather than reduce the absorption of noise by stock prices. In this case, even neoclassical capital markets will fail to aggregate and transmit large amounts of scattered knowledge.

Contrary to scattered knowledge, insider knowledge is not dispersed throughout society. Access to the information sources of insider knowledge is limited. Only a small number of investors will be able to acquire or generate insider knowledge. If the total number of capital market participants is large, as is the case in neoclassical capital markets, most of the information which is incorporated by market prices as a result of insider transactions will be offset by liquidity trades and uninformed speculation.

Under neoclassical regulation, the amount of insider knowledge incorporated by stock prices is even further reduced by strict laws against insider trading. Well-enforced prohibition of insider trading reduces the incentives to search for and trade on the basis of unpublished event information. Consequently, smaller amounts of event information will be incorporated and transmitted by price signals.

While insider event information which causes price increases is likely to be published by corporate insiders and subsequently incorporated and transmitted by security prices, insider event information which may cause price declines is likely to be kept secret. Consider, for example, major decision errors by corporate executives. Under weak insider regulations, corporate executives are likely to hedge themselves against potential losses in human capital by trading on the basis of their insider knowledge with regard to these decision errors. Strict laws against insider trading, on the other hand, will prevent the diffusion of event information through the price mechanism.

Neoclassical regulation discourages investors from holding undiversified portfolios and invest in corporate governance. Extensive, well-specified and strictly enforced accounting, disclosure and auditing rules reduce the information and governance advantages associated with ownership concentration. Strict laws against insider trading prevent active investors from recovering nondiversification costs. As a result, corporate ownership is highly fragmented. Corporate governance relies on the disciplinary effects of an active market for corporate control. Anti-takeover regulation, however, protects incumbent management against hostile takeovers. Without an active market for corporate control, unintermediated neoclassical capital markets cannot provide strong governance structures. Consequently, corporate managers are well entrenched.

Relational capital markets

Relational regulation discourages non-insiders from participating in capital market transactions. The total number of capital market participants remains relatively low under relational regulation. Consequently, relational capital markets cannot aggregate and transmit large amounts of scattered knowledge.

On the other hand, relational capital markets are able to aggregate larger amounts of insider knowledge and transmit insider knowledge more accurately than neoclassical capital markets. No laws or weak laws against insider trading encourage investors to search for and trade on the basis of unpublished event information. Corporate executives will try to hedge themselves against decision errors by trading on the basis of negative event information. Non-insiders are confronted with substantial information disadvantages. Hence they will either prefer long-term investment strategies or refrain from participating in capital market transactions at all. Under these circumstances, insiders will account for a relatively large portion of total trading volume. Liquidity trades and uninformed speculation are less likely to offset most of the insider knowledge which is incorporated by stock prices.

Corporate governance within relational capital markets does not rely on the disciplinary effects of an active market for corporate control. Relational regulation encourages investors to forego risk diversification in favor of ownership concentration. Large active investors enjoy substantial information advantages. In addition, they are able to recover nondiversification costs via insider trading. Investors holding large percentages of a corporation's outstanding shares do not only possess strong incentives to invest into corporate governance, they are also able to initiate the replacement of inefficient management teams.

Investment companies and investment trusts

Basic features Investment companies and investment trusts sell share certificates to savers and invest the proceeds in a (usually diversified) portfolio of securities. Investment companies are characterized by the fact that the participating parties constitute a company under company law. Each share certificate issued by an investment company represents a proportionate interest in the company's assets and profits. Investment trusts are composed of an advisor who gives instructions regarding the operation of the trust property, a trustee who administers the trust property in accordance with the instructions received from the advisor, and the beneficiaries. The participating parties of an investment trust do not constitute a company under company law. The relationship between advisor, trustee and beneficiaries is governed by contracts.

There are two kinds of investment companies: closed-end funds and open-end funds. The latter are more popularly referred to as mutual funds. Shares of closed-end funds are sold in the primary market and subsequently traded in secondary markets like any other kind of stock. A closed-end investment company has no obligation to redeem its shares. An open-end or mutual fund, on the other hand, continuously offers new shares to the public and has to commit itself to redeem outstanding shares at their current net asset value. The net asset value of a share is determined by dividing the market value of the entire portfolio by the number of outstanding shares.

Investment companies consist of an advisor, an administrator and a board of directors. The investment company's portfolio is exclusively managed by a specialized advisor, who buys and sells securities on behalf of the shareholders. All other activities which are necessary to create and operate a fund are performed by an administrator. The board members are elected at the shareholder meeting. The board's main task is to protect shareholder interests. The board is entitled to approve and terminate advisory contracts. Although funds may contract external advisors, there are many cases in which advisor, administrator and even some of the board members are employed by the same investment organization.

Shares of investment companies may be sold either directly or through a specialized sales force. To cover marketing and distribution costs, investment companies can charge a commission for share purchase (the so-called load) or a redemption fee (back-end load). Even if the investment company does not carry any load it still may cover its marketing costs by an annual fee taken out of the fund's assets. In addition, the investment company's assets are continuously reduced by advisory and administration fees as well as transaction costs resulting from security trades.

There are two kinds of investment trusts: unit trusts and open trusts. Unit trusts are characterized by a fixed number of unit certificates, a fixed termination date and the absence of active trading within the portfolio. After the unit trust has been assembled by the so-called sponsor, it is turned over to a trustee who holds all securities (usually bonds) until they are redeemed by the issuer. Only in case of a dramatic decline in the issuer's creditworthiness is the trustee entitled to sell premature securities. Unlike unit trusts, open trusts may issue additional certificates, can have an indefinite as well as a definite termination date and are usually engaged in an active portfolio management. In case of an indefinite termination date, share certificates are usually redeemable at net asset value.

Investment companies and investment trusts may restrict themselves to invest only in securities of a special kind, e.g. bonds, industry (e.g. telecommunications), territory (e.g. South-East Asia), company size (e.g. small caps), risk level (e.g. low-risk), etc. Some investment companies and trusts prefer to invest in a prespecified combination of various types of securities (e.g. 50 percent stocks,

50 percent bonds). The overall investment objective may be either growth, income or any combination thereof. Growth funds directly reinvest all returns, whereas income funds aim at providing shareholders with a stable flow of income.

Knowledge utilization Can fund intermediation improve the allocation of scarce capital? The answer to this question depends upon (1) the kind and amount of knowledge on which fund advisors base their investment decisions, and (2) the division of investment decisions between savers and fund advisors.

(1) Effect information represents the area in which fund advisors enjoy the largest information advantage over ordinary investors. Professional training, specialized skills, investment experience and a qualified support staff enable fund advisors to base their investment decisions on more sophisticated effect information than ordinary investors. Based on sophisticated effect information, fund advisors are able to use available event information more effectively than ordinary investors. Although fund advisors have no comparative advantage over ordinary investors with respect to the acquisition of public information, superior effect knowledge enables fund advisors to interpret public information, especially when it is incomplete, more accurately than ordinary investors. For the same reason, fragmentary insider knowledge is more valuable to fund advisors than to ordinary investors.

Whether investment companies and investment trusts possess comparative advantages over ordinary investors with respect to insider information depends upon the prevailing regulatory environment. Under neoclassical regulation, strict diversification requirements preclude investment companies and investment trusts from becoming corporate insiders by acquiring concentrated ownership rights. Even if fund advisors were able to acquire insider information, strict laws against insider trading would preclude them from trading on the basis of their insider knowledge. However, the enforcement of neoclassical insider restrictions is usually limited to insider trading on the basis of specific event information. Regulators cannot effectively prohibit insider trading on the basis of unspecific or fragmentary insider knowledge. Consequently, fund intermediation partly enhances the ability of neoclassical capital markets to aggregate and transmit (fragmentary and unspecific) insider knowledge.

Relational regulation, on the other hand, does not impose strict diversification requirements on financial intermediaries. Investment companies and investment trusts may become corporate insiders by acquiring concentrated ownership rights. Nonexistent or weak laws against insider trading allow investment companies and investment trusts to benefit from their insider knowledge. As a result, fund intermediation enhances the informational efficiency of relational capital markets with respect to the aggregation and transmission of insider knowledge.

(2) The division of investment decisions between savers and fund advisors is determined by a fund's degree of specialization. Unspecialized funds relieve savers from any investment responsibility. Advisors of general funds must decide in which sectors, industries, countries, corporations and securities the accumulated savings will be invested. Capital allocation relies exclusively upon the experience and knowledge which has been acquired by fund advisors and their support staff. Highly specialized funds, on the other hand, impose large amounts of investment responsibility on savers. By selecting specialized funds, savers allocate their capital to certain sectors, industries, territories, etc., whereas fund advisors are limited to allocating the accumulated resources within their fund's investment focus. By selecting among different kinds of funds, savers are able to combine their often fragmentary and scattered knowledge with the sophisticated effect knowledge of professional fund advisors.

Risk diversification   Fund intermediation enhances risk diversification by realizing economies of scale with respect to transaction costs. Since security trades cause volume-independent transaction costs, small investors are confronted with prohibitively high transaction costs when trying to diversify their portfolios' unsystematic risk. Unlike small investors, investment companies and investment trusts accumulate large amounts of capital. The size of their financial resources enables investment companies and investment trusts to realize economies of scale with respect to volume-independent transaction costs and to diversify their portfolios more completely than small investors. By diversifying unsystematic risk, fund intermediation eliminates the high-risk differential between common stock and other forms of investment (Friend *et al.* 1970: 22). As a result, fund intermediation reduces the costs of equity. Small investors no longer have to incur the risk of holding an incompletely diversified portfolio when investing in common stock.

Agency costs Fund intermediation enhances corporate governance within neoclassical capital markets. Unlike small investors, investment companies and investment trusts are able to earn positive returns from investments into corporate governance. Investment companies and investment trusts acquire larger amounts of a corporation's outstanding liabilities than small investors. Thus investment companies and investment trusts are able to internalize a larger share of governance benefits than individual savers. Investments into corporate governance become even more attractive when several funds which have invested in the same corporation constitute a jointly managed fund family. In this case, each individual fund is able to fulfill the diversification requirements imposed by neoclassical regulation without attenuating the incentives to invest into corporate governance.

As well-trained professionals, fund advisors will exercise corporate governance more effectively than small investors. Based on their education, experience and the information provided by a qualified support staff, fund advisors can assess corporate performance more accurately than ordinary investors.

Fund intermediation also reduces signaling costs. Signaling creditworthiness to an anonymous variety of individual savers is far more expensive than convincing a group of fund advisors. Furthermore, fund intermediation creates some privacy within an investment relationship, enabling entrepreneurs to signal firm-specific information to fund advisors without automatically disclosing it to potential competitors.

So far, the analysis has been focused on potential benefits of fund intermediation. However, the benefits of fund intermediation may be offset by additional agency costs. The shareholder–advisor/administrator relationship is a typical principal–agent relationship. The actions of fund advisors, especially their investment decisions, determine shareholder wealth. Because of information asymmetries and sunk costs, fund advisors and administrators may be in a position to take actions which are to their personal benefit, yet not in the best interest of shareholders. The potential spectrum of such opportunistic behavior is rather wide. It includes excessive administration cost charges, commission-induced portfolio turnovers and acceptance of low takeover bids.[27] In the absence of any disciplinary forces, shareholders must fear that fund advisors and/or administrators will try to transfer shareholder wealth either directly or via third parties into their own pockets.

Opportunism within principal–agent relations may be restricted by incentive alignment, monitoring, or competition. If institutional arrangements can be designed which align the interests of fund advisors/administrators and shareholders, all agency problems will disappear. Performance-based compensation plans and ownership rights have the potential to serve as incentive alignment devices in many principal–agent situations. However, both face serious limitations in the case of fund intermediation. Compensating fund advisors according to the performance of the fund's portfolio would induce them to favor risky investments, because they would fully benefit from increasing expected returns, whereas the additional risk would affect them only partially.[28] These incentive asymmetries would disappear if fund advisors/administrators held shares of the funds which they manage/administrate. The willingness of fund advisors/administrators to invest into their own funds would signal that they do not intend to exploit shareholders. However, fund advisors/administrators rarely possess enough financial resources to credibly signal their good intentions. In fact, limited financial resources have been the reason why they became agents.

Since large investors realize most of the benefits provided by funds without incurring additional agency costs of fund intermediation, shareholders of investment companies and investment trusts are typically small investors. Thus monitoring of fund advisors/administrators by shareholders will be extremely weak. Individual cost-benefit calculations will keep most shareholders from attending annual shareholder meetings. As a consequence, a majority of voting rights will be controlled by fund managers through proxy voting rights (Wharton School 1962: 8). Because of this "proxy machinery" most boards of directors consist of individuals who are affiliated with or selected by the fund advisor/administrator (Friend *et al.* 1970: 28–9). This minimizes the probability that any of the advisor's decisions will be questioned by the board. Moreover, the board's right to replace advisors remains a theoretical threat.

Competitive forces eliminate excessive agency costs by removing scarce resources from inefficient to efficient competitors. Effective competition is based on contestable markets and the absence of lock-in situations. Contestable markets allow new competitors to enter without any restrictions and without incurring sunk costs (Baumol *et al.* 1988). Since neither significant entry restrictions nor major sunk costs prevail in the fund industry, fund markets are highly contestable.[29] As a consequence, incumbent fund advisors/

administrators who charge excessive fees or try to exploit share-holders otherwise have to fear that new competitors will enter the fund industry and attract shareholders by refraining from shareholder exploitation. However, market contestability alone is not sufficient to restrict opportunism. If shareholders cannot withdraw their capital from inefficient investment companies and investment trusts because they find themselves in a lock-in situation, competitive forces will be impaired.

The shareholders' ability to withdraw their resources from ineffi-cient funds depends upon the kind of investment companies and investment trusts which are involved. Closed-end funds and unit trusts do not allow shareholders to directly remove their invested capital. Shareholders who are not satisfied with the performance of a closed-end fund can only sell their shares in secondary markets. Since these sales do not reduce the current amount of capital accu-mulated by the fund, advisors and administrators are not immediately affected. However, the price decrease caused by these sales will dete-riorate the conditions under which the investment company will be able to raise new capital for future investment purposes. Additionally, declining share prices in the secondary market will result in a loss of the fund advisor's/administrator's reputation.

Open-end funds and open trusts, on the other hand, have to redeem outstanding shares on demand on the basis of the fund's net asset value. Since share redemption directly reduces the amount of capital which is available to the investment company or investment trust, advisors and administrators of mutual funds and open trusts are confronted with a continuous liquidity threat. In order to reduce this threat, mutual funds and open trusts may try to introduce load charges, either in form of sales commissions or redemption fees. Both front-end and back-end load charges will dilute shareholder mobility by increasing the bid–ask spread. Front-end loads force investors to incur sunk costs whereas back-end loads create exit barriers. However, competition between load and low-load or no-load funds limits the restrictions of shareholder mobility to be imposed by load charges. Moreover, modern redemption procedures such as Internet transfers reduce the transaction costs of switching from inefficient to efficient funds.

Whereas competition governs the principal–agent relationship between shareholders and fund advisors/administrators in closed-end investment companies and unit trusts solely through the performance incentives provided by reputational effects and future conditions of capital acquisition, the combination of share redemption and high degrees of shareholder mobility adds more immediate market forces to restrict agency costs in open-end funds and open trusts. Hence the agency costs emerging from the shareholder–fund advisor/administrator relationship are substantially less in open-end funds and open trusts than in closed-end funds and unit trusts.

Banks

There are three basic kinds of banks: commercial banks, investment banks and universal banks. Commercial banks are restricted to depository and lending activities. Investment banks typically engage in underwriting activities, securities trading, fund management and merger and acquisition services. Universal banks combine the activities of commercial and investment banks under one roof.

Commercial banks

Basic features The main economic functions of commercial banks are reflected by the structure of their balance sheet. Deposits, equity, and loans granted by other financial institutions appear on the liability side of a bank's balance sheet, whereas assets are composed of loans (both to customers and financial institutions) and reserves. Based on the structure of their balance sheet, the economic activities of commercial banks can be divided into four categories: liquidity services, liability services, asset services and transformation services.

The liquidity services which commercial banks provide for their creditors include deposit holding, interest payment, transaction clearing, currency exchange and a wide variety of additional services which are associated with different forms of non-cash payments. The liability services provided to equity owners depend upon the legal structure of the bank. In the case of a publicly held corporation, maximizing the market value of outstanding shares will be the primary objective. Asset services focus on the provision of loans to borrowers in exchange for interest payments. Transformation services are necessary to meet the different demands of depositors and borrowers.[30] Commercial banks usually receive a large number of small-sized, short-term and highly liquid assets from risk-averse depositors which have to be transformed into a smaller number of

51

large-sized, long-term, illiquid and risky loans. Hence transformation services include size, maturity, liquidity and risk transformation.

Size transformation is necessary because the size of bank loans is usually larger than the size of individual bank deposits. Banks accumulate the deposits of many individuals in order to provide borrowers with the desired amount of debt. Since size transformation can be achieved without financial intermediation by simply breaking down large loans into a number of small-sized loans, size transformation in itself cannot explain the emergence of commercial banks.

Maturity transformation describes the process of financing long-lived assets (e.g. loans to non-banks) with short-term liabilities (e.g. deposits). By providing maturity transformation services, commercial banks facilitate the realization of long-term investment projects. Long-term debt provides entrepreneurs who plan to invest in long-term investment projects with a stable financial basis. Without maturity transformation, entrepreneurs would be confronted with high—often prohibitively high—financial uncertainties.

The long-term interest rates charged by commercial banks include a premium which compensates the bank for its maturity transformation service. Maturity transformation makes commercial banks vulnerable to unexpected interest rate changes. However, specialization and consolidation enables commercial banks to keep the costs which result from unexpected interest rate changes at a low level.

Commercial banks are highly specialized intermediaries who continuously screen capital market developments. Professional training, industry experience and specialized skills enable bank managers to forecast interest rate changes with high accuracy and at lower costs than corporate executives who are mainly engaged in production or other nonfinancial activities. Consequently, commercial banks will be less often exposed to unexpected interest rate changes than their borrowers would be without bank intermediation.

Consolidation describes the process of risk reduction through the accumulation of independent risk.[31] Accumulating a large number of loans with different maturity dates reduces the overall risk associated with unexpected interest rate changes. The economic effects of unexpected interest rate fluctuations are likely to offset each other within a large portfolio of independent loans. Due to the effects of risk consolidation, commercial banks can handle unexpected interest rate changes more effectively than individual borrowers. In short, commercial banks convert financial instability into financial stability through specialization and risk consolidation.

Commercial banks create liquidity by transforming illiquid assets (loans) into liquid liabilities (deposits). Asset liquidity is measured by two dimensions: first, the time it takes to find somebody who is willing to pay money in exchange for the respective asset, and second, the loss of value which the original owner has to incur as a result of this exchange. According to this definition, asset maturity and asset liquidity seem to be inseparable characteristics. However, asset liquidity and asset maturity can be clearly distinguished from each other. The former focuses on premature liquidation, whereas the latter refers exclusively to the regular expiration of lending contracts.

Bank loans are usually highly illiquid. This illiquidity results from the evaluation problems which are associated with bank loans. Since each bank loan has unique characteristics, there is no common market price for bank loans. Before granting a loan, commercial banks screen the borrower's financial and economic situation. After granting a loan, commercial banks monitor the borrower's financial and economic development. Due to these screening and monitoring activities, commercial banks possess insider information about the current value of their loans. Since commercial banks cannot credibly convey their insider knowledge to outsiders, potential buyers of bank loans must always fear that the asking price exceeds the loan's real value. Thus bank loans are highly illiquid, non-tradeable assets. Bank deposits, on the other side, are equally untradeable, yet highly liquid assets. Except for minor restrictions, depositors are entitled to withdraw their deposits at any time.[32]

The fourth transformation function performed by commercial banks is risk transformation. Although it may seem at first glance as if risk and illiquidity refer to the same characteristics of an asset, both dimensions can be clearly distinguished. Liquid assets are not automatically riskless, and vice versa.[33] A stock option, for example, is a highly liquid yet extremely risky investment, whereas real estate is usually an illiquid but riskless asset. Risk transformation involves (1) the conversion of high-risk assets (loans) into low-risk liabilities (deposits), and (2) the reduction of the default risk associated with bank loans.

(1) The transformation of high-risk loans into low-risk deposits is based on risk diversification and deposit insurance. Diamond (1984: 404–7) identifies two forms of risk diversification: risk aggregation

and risk sharing. Risk aggregation does not reduce the risk of bank deposits. A single bank which invests in an increasing number of loans accumulates rather than reduces default risk. Since there is only one bank, this bank has to bear the entire default risk of each loan. An increasing number of loans does not reduce the overall default risk, but rather exposes the bank to additional default risk. Risk sharing, on the other hand, involves n banks, each of which spreads its funds across N loans. The larger n and N, the lower will be the fraction which each bank invests in a single loan. Since each independent loan risk will be shared by an increasing number of banks, risk sharing reduces the overall risk incurred by each individual bank and its depositors. Most of the remaining default risk can be eliminated through deposit insurance.

(2) In an unintermediated capital market, creditors will invest either too little or too much into screening and monitoring activities. If screening and monitoring costs are high in relation to the resulting benefits, creditors will try to free-ride on the screening and monitoring activities of fellow creditors. Under-investment will be the inevitable consequence. If screening and monitoring costs are low in relation to the resulting benefits, too many creditors will perform screening and monitoring activities. Over-investment will be the consequence. Both over- and under-investment can be prevented through financial intermediation.

Financial intermediaries who specialize in corporate screening and monitoring will be confronted with the deficiencies of information markets, when they try to sell the information generated through screening and monitoring activities to creditors. Since information markets suffer from quality uncertainty, financial intermediaries incur high signaling costs in order to sell their information. After the information has been sold, it can easily be multiplied and resold by others. As a result, financial intermediaries will be unable to earn positive returns from their screening and monitoring activities by selling the resulting information. However, financial intermediaries can earn positive returns if they produce low-risk asset claims based on their screening and monitoring activities and sell these low-risk asset claims instead of trying to sell their information directly (Leland and Pyle 1977: 383). Low-risk asset claims eliminate the problems associated with quality uncertainty and cannot be multiplied.

Commercial banks do not try to sell the information acquired through screening and monitoring activities. Instead, they use this information to transform high-risk bank loans into low-risk deposits. By selling low-risk deposit claims at a premium, commercial banks are able to earn positive returns from their screening and monitoring investments.

Knowledge utilization   Commercial banks allocate capital on the basis of more accurate event information and more sophisticated effect information than ordinary investors. According to Nakamura (1991), commercial banks obtain private event information about a corporation's financial and economic situation by observing checking account transactions. Ordinary investors do not have access to this information source which provides commercial banks with important insider information. Since insider restrictions are limited to capital market transactions, relational regulation does not preclude commercial banks from granting or denying loans on the basis of insider knowledge. Professional training, specialized skills and lending experience enable bank executives to combine their insider advantages with superior effect information. These information advantages enhance allocative efficiency and reduce the costs of financial distress.

Since the economic value of a firm is not only determined by its current financial situation, but to a large extent by future investment opportunities which result from the firm's specific asset combination (Myers 1977), bankruptcy procedures bear the risk of destroying economic values. The resulting costs are larger within unintermediated than within bank intermediated capital markets. Commercial banks can forecast a firm's prospective earnings more accurately than ordinary creditors, and possess the necessary resources to help a firm overcome financial distress. In addition, bank intermediation reduces the coordination problems associated with restructuring loans to financially distressed firms. As Berlin and Mester (1992) point out, contract renegotiation with a small number of well-informed intermediaries is less costly than with an anonymous plurality of lenders in an unintermediated capital market.

Moreover, bank intermediation reduces signaling costs. The costs of signaling low default risk within unintermediated capital markets are often prohibitively high. Firms have to convince a large number of potential creditors who do not necessarily possess advanced financial skills. Bank intermediation facilitates signaling by guaranteeing qualified signal interpretation and avoiding unnecessary multiplication of signaling efforts.

If a signal serves as a perfect substitute for *ex ante* screening and *ex post* monitoring, bank executives may reward the respective borrower by charging lower interest rates. The resulting price discrimination enables some firms which would otherwise be subjected to credit rationing to realize their investment projects. But commercial banks cannot eliminate the problem of credit rationing. Since commercial banks are precluded from exercising non-default decision rights, they are limited in their ability to control the default risk of their loans.

Risk diversification   Commercial banks enhance risk diversification via risk sharing. Since commercial banks accumulate large amounts of capital, they are able to diversify their loan risk via risk sharing more completely than individual investors. In addition to risk diversification, overall default risk is further reduced through risk transformation.

Agency costs   Bank intermediation eliminates unnecessary multiplication of screening and monitoring activities, and internalizes screening and monitoring benefits more completely than unintermediated capital markets. The process of risk transformation creates strong incentives for commercial banks to invest in screening and monitoring activities. Commercial banks have to bear the entire default risk associated with their loans, whereas depositors hold almost riskless deposit claims. However, the screening and monitoring activities of commercial banks are limited to the reduction of default risk.

Investment banks

Basic features   Investment banks are primarily engaged in public offerings, private placements, financial innovation, securities trading, portfolio management and merger and acquisition assistance. Public offerings include stock as well as bond issues. Stock issues may involve initial or seasoned public offerings. Unintermediated equity markets cannot effectively reduce the information asymmetries associated with initial public offerings. Uninformed investors who bid for initial public offerings will continuously receive excessive shares of overpriced issues, because informed investors will enter the bidding process only if they expect the offer to be underpriced. Issuers, on the other hand, cannot credibly signal the true value of their offerings. Without investment bank intermediation these problems will lead to a breakdown of primary equity markets.

Although investment banks cannot completely eliminate the information asymmetries associated with initial public offerings, they are able to prevent a market breakdown by reducing these information asymmetries to a reasonable level. Investment banks are involved in many initial public offerings over time. Continuous market presence enables them to develop a reputation. Since investment banks earn reputation rents, they have strong incentives to maintain their good reputation. Investment banks will try to acquire accurate information about an issuing firm's economic and financial perspectives, and will try to ask equilibrium offer prices. Investment bankers who ask higher prices than the equilibrium price will lose customers on the investors' side; bankers who ask prices which are below the equilibrium price will have trouble acquiring new customers among issuing firms.

According to Rock (1986) and Beatty and Ritter (1986), the equilibrium price of a bank-intermediated initial public offering lies below the issue's expected secondary market price. Despite investment bank intermediation, there are still two kinds of investors in the market: informed and uninformed investors. Informed investors will crowd out uninformed investors whenever they expect to gain from underpriced offerings. Uninformed investors will anticipate this problem and will submit bids only if they can expect average investment returns from initial public offerings. Average investment returns to uninformed investors imply that the average initial public offering is underpriced, because uninformed investors receive a disproportionately high share of overpriced issues. The underpricing equilibrium guarantees uninformed investors an average investment return, whereas informed investors earn excessive returns which compensate them for their information costs.

Besides enhancing the functioning of primary equity markets, investment banks provide important distribution and insurance services. Specialized and continuously reemployed distribution channels allow investment banks to sell new issues faster and at lower marketing costs than ordinary issuers. Insurance costs are kept low by the formation of syndicates among investment banks and by book-building prior to the offering. Syndication allows investment banks, which are already engaged in a large number of issues, to further diversify issuing risk (Ramakrishnan and Thakor

1984). Book-building reduces market uncertainties in a way usually not realizable by the issuing firm itself.

The amount of insurance provided by an investment bank depends upon the form of underwriting contract which has been chosen. In a "firm commitment" contract, the investment banker purchases the entire issue at a fixed price and tries to resell it in the market place. All uncertainties about future price developments in the primary market and, if the investment bank fails to sell the whole issue right away, in the secondary market are covered by the underwriting bank.[34] A "best efforts" contract does not bind the bank to buy any of the issued securities. The bank acts solely as a marketing agent, using its skill and distribution channels to sell as many securities as possible. This agreement usually contains a clause which allows issuing corporations to cancel the offering if less than a prespecified amount of securities has been sold within a certain period of time. In case of a "best efforts" contract, the entire risk has to be borne by the issuing firm. A "standby" contract binds the underwriter to purchase all securities which remain unsold. Since the prespecified price at which the bank has to buy unsold shares is considerably lower than the initial asking price, market uncertainties are in fact shared by the issuer and the investment banker. For its distribution and insurance services the investment bank either charges a fee or keeps the spread between the public offering price and the price paid to the issuing corporation.

The different forms of underwriting schemes enable each issuing firm to adjust the combination of distribution and insurance services to its individual needs (see Mandelker and Raviv 1977). From the viewpoint of the investment bank, the contractual flexibility offers the chance to design self-selection mechanisms which automatically reduce existing information asymmetries at very low costs.[35]

Seasoned equity issues may be marketed through rights offerings instead of using the services of an investment bank. In a rights offering, each shareholder receives an option to buy new shares. Usually, one right is issued for each outstanding share. The issuing corporation has to state the number of rights which are necessary in order for entitlement to purchase one unit of the new security, the exercise price and the expiration date of the option. Since stocks of the issuing corporation are already traded in the market, seasoned equity offerings involve less severe information asymmetries than initial public offerings. Stock price reactions to the announcement of issuing new securities convey information about the market's perception of the offering. In addition, price reactions effectively constrain incumbent owners not to exploit investors by issuing new equity at unfavorable terms. Moreover, trading of the rights to purchase new securities generates and transmits further information to potential investors and employs market forces to allocate new securities. Although unintermediated capital markets have the potential of reducing all information-related problems to a reasonable limit, issuing corporations may still prefer a (more expensive) underwritten offering in order to benefit from the distribution and insurance services provided by investment banks.

Investment bank intermediated bond issues provide an alternative to unintermediated bond issues and bank loans. Compared to unintermediated bond issues, investment bank intermediation reduces signaling costs, guarantees an efficient level of corporate screening and provides distribution and insurance services. Unlike commercial banks, investment banks do not engage in *ex post* monitoring. Consequently, investment bank intermediated bond issues are only attractive if investors do not have to control default risk through monitoring activities.

Private placements are an efficient way of issuing debt or equity when a small number of investors are willing to acquire the entire issue. Private placements cause less administration and marketing costs than public offerings. Since each investor buys a major share of the issue, an efficient level of *ex ante* screening and *ex post* monitoring is assured. Nevertheless, investment banks may be contracted to assist the placement. As Carey *et al.* (1993: 33) note, investment banks may add value in several ways. They reduce search costs by acting as brokers, i.e. by screening issues and matching them with investors who possess compatible preferences. Issuers and investors not maintaining continuous market presence prefer to purchase pricing services from investment banks instead of gathering the required information themselves, especially if they have no comparable capital market prices to refer to. Furthermore, investment banks reduce transaction costs by enforcing informal bargaining and contract execution conventions.

The most important function of investment banks is the creation of new financial tools. Most of the recent financial innovations have first been introduced by investment banks to institutional investors in the private placement market. Financial innovations promote economic growth by improving capital allocation and/or corporate governance.

Important trading services provided by investment banks include market-making for recently issued securities and block-trading. By acting as market-makers for a limited period of time after the initial offering, investment banks guarantee a high level of market liquidity in otherwise relatively thin markets. Investors will honor these market-making activities by purchasing larger shares of the initial offering.

Trading of more than 10,000 shares of a single security is referred to as block trading. Unintermediated capital markets usually cannot absorb block orders without severe price-reactions. Block sales may either be liquidity- or information-induced. Since investors cannot verify the true motives of a block offer, they will be reluctant to pay current market prices. Block buys, on the other hand, are always information-induced, because nobody has to buy large amounts of a single security solely for liquidity reasons.[36] Investment bankers may assist block traders by building a syndicate of investors who are willing to buy (respectively sell) sub-blocks. As a result of the syndication process, both sides of the trade will be better off than they would have been in an unintermediated market. Block traders will benefit from superior price conditions, while syndicate members will save on transaction costs.[37]

Most investment banks expand their activities to portfolio and fund management in order to benefit from the information gathered in connection with public offerings and private placements. This information cannot be directly sold because of prohibitively high signaling costs. Incorporating this information into portfolio and fund management services, on the other hand, enables investment banks to sell their information indirectly.

Market insight and evaluation experience qualify investment banks to provide merger and acquisition assistance. Screening activities and continuous market observation enable investment banks to identify undervalued firms as takeover candidates. The presence of investment banks guarantees the provision of takeover information even if other market participants refrain from generating this kind of information because of free-riding problems.

Investment bank intermediation reduces suspicion on both sides of a takeover. Target shareholders are usually reluctant to accept takeover bids which are presented directly by the acquiring firm. Investment bank intermediated bids usually earn a higher rate of acceptance. Based on their reputation, investment banks are able, first, to convince target shareholders that they receive a reasonable price for their shares, and second, to assure owners of the acquiring firm that the takeover is efficiency driven and not the result of managerial discretion.

Investment banks may further support mergers and acquisitions through risk arbitrage and assistance in raising the amount of capital which is necessary to submit successful takeover bids. Investment banks which engage in risk arbitrage in association with takeover bids acquire a long position in the target firm and a short position in the bidding firm. Since the position taken in the target firm will be tendered to the bidder if the takeover is successful, risk arbitrage reduces the problem of free-riding by target firm shareholders.

Knowledge utilization   Investment bank intermediation promotes allocative efficiency through financial innovation and by reinstalling and enhancing capital market forces. Investment banks try to earn innovation rents by developing new financial instruments which enhance allocative efficiency. The process of innovation and subsequent imitation continuously improves the performance of investment bank intermediated capital markets.

Although investment bank intermediation successfully prevents a breakdown of primary equity markets by reducing information asymmetries to reasonable levels, some inefficiencies will remain. Above all, investment bank intermediation cannot eliminate the prevailing underpricing equilibrium which imposes a cost premium on equity.[38]

Risk diversification   Investment banks diversify the risk associated with public offerings via syndication and book-building. In addition, investment bank intermediation promotes the development and distribution of new instruments for risk diversification. For example, options, futures and swaps have been introduced by investment banks.

Agency costs   The direct contributions of investment banks to the reduction of agency costs are limited to *ex ante* screening activities. Investment bank intermediation prevents unnecessary multiplication of screening costs and eliminates free-riding problems. Reputational effects guarantee that investment banks possess strong incentives to act in their customers' best interests (see Chemmanur and Fulghieri 1994).

Although investment banks do not directly engage in *ex post* monitoring, they indirectly contribute to corporate governance via financial innovation and by facilitating corporate takeovers. Investment bank intermediated capital markets are usually characterized by more active markets for corporate control than unintermediated capital markets.

Universal banks

Universal banks may be divided into ordinary and privileged universal banks. Ordinary universal banks engage in commercial and investment banking, but do not exercise control over non-banks. Privileged universal banks engage in commercial and investment banking and exercise control over non-banks through equity ownership, proxy voting and board representation.

Ordinary universal banks

Basic features   Ordinary universal banks will enjoy quality and/or cost advantages over commercial and investment banks whenever the information acquired in the credit and deposit business is of significant value to activities undertaken in the investment business and vice versa. In the commercial sector, banks continuously gain valuable insight into the financial and economic situation of their customers when providing them with deposit and credit services. While commercial banks are restricted to using this information for loan purposes, universal banks extend the application of credit and deposit information to investment-related decisions. Consequently, investment banks which compete with universal banks have to acquire this knowledge through other channels or build their investment decisions on a less solid informational foundation. The former will result in cost disadvantages, the latter in quality disadvantages. Although the application of investment-related information to the commercial business may be less obvious at first sight, important synergies do exist. Consider, for example, that the information which has been generated through screening activities in the underwriting business reduces the costs of evaluating loan risk.

Conflicts of interests will occur within universal banks wherever the services which are demanded by customers in one line of business threaten to impair profits which are earned in another line. A closer look at the sources of profits of ordinary universal banks will reveal these conflicts of interest. In the commercial banking business, the largest source of profits are interest payments which banks receive in association with their loans. Commissions and underwriting fees represent the major sources of profit in the investment banking business.

Conflicts of interest arise with regard to bank loans and underwriting activities. Every dollar lent to a firm reduces the potential amount of fees to be earned by providing underwriting services to the same firm and vice versa. The continuous flow of profits generated by commercial lending usually exceeds the profits which can be earned by comparable underwriting activities. The information created by screening and monitoring activities enables a bank to earn information rents in the credit business. Whenever a loan agreement has to be renegotiated, the original lender, based on his or her idiosyncratic knowledge, enjoys a significant cost advantage over rival lenders who do not possess insider knowledge about the specific default risk. Thus competitors cannot provide the loan at the same favorable terms as the original lender.

The information generated in relation with underwriting activities, on the other hand, does not generate a stream of information rents. The information is usually corporate-specific and loses its value as soon as the underwriting process has been completed. Due to this asymmetry, ordinary universal banks will try to sell bank loans instead of underwriting activities to their customers, even if their customers were better off by raising capital via public offerings.[39] To what extent ordinary universal banks will succeed in their effort to withhold firms from raising capital in primary markets depends upon the competitive setting within the banking sector which, in turn, is determined by the prevailing regulatory environment.

Within a regulatory environment which allows investment, commercial and universal banks to coexist, domestic investment and commercial banks will be crowded out by domestic ordinary universal banks. Information cost advantages enable domestic universal banks to provide investment as well as commercial banking services at lower costs than rival domestic banks which concentrate their activities in one line of business. After crowding out rival domestic investment and commercial banks, the surviving universal banks will tend to shift their focus to the more profitable lending business. Firms that prefer to raise funds in the capital market will experience increasing bank resistance, especially if these firms are small and possess little bargaining power.

The bank which provides underwriting services at the lowest cost is the firm's main lending bank. Since this bank would lose its information rent by providing the firm with underwriting services, it has little incentive to do so. Another bank would have to acquire firm-specific knowledge before being able to offer underwriting services. After having acquired firm-specific knowledge, however, this bank also has strong incentives to earn a continuous stream of information rents by providing the firm with renegotiable bank loans instead of earning one-off underwriting fees. Without strong competition from foreign (neoclassically regulated) investment banks, domestic ordinary universal banks will succeed in forcing dependent customers to refrain from raising funds in the capital market by threatening to recall loans or increase interest rates.

Knowledge utilization   Contrary to investment banks, ordinary universal banks impair capital market forces. Capital markets which are intermediated by ordinary universal banks will fail to aggregate and transmit large amounts of scattered knowledge. The success of universal banks in withholding firms from issuing securities in capital markets will lead to an erosion of investment banking. After an economy's investment banking sector has eroded, efforts to reactivate investment banking will fail due to prohibitively high knowledge and reputation barriers. As a consequence, capital markets will be underdeveloped, primary equity markets will break down, financial innovation will cease, firms will be dependent on bank loans and ordinary universal banks will earn high information rents. Competition among universal banks may enable some firms to capture a part of these information rents in the form of lower interest rates. However, this benefit will be offset by an overall increase in capital costs due to the underdevelopment of capital markets.

Risk diversification   The integration of commercial and investment banking may lead to adverse risk effects. Universal banking is often accused of creating incentives and opportunities to invest customer deposits in high-risk securities.[40] But why should universal banks have more incentives than commercial banks to increase their expected profits by taking high default risk?

Without deposit insurance, universal and commercial banks have to bear the entire default risk of their investments. As a result they will have the same (dis)incentive to engage in high-risk investments. If deposits are insured, the incentive of commercial and universal banks to take high risk will increase, because they do not have to bear the entire default risk. In this case, however, the incentive to invest deposits in high-risk securities is created by deposit insurance, not by universal banking. Of course, commercial banks do not have the opportunity to invest customer deposits in corporate securities. But they do have the opportunity to increase their expected profits by charging higher interest rates in exchange for high-risk loans.

In addition, universal banking may destabilize the financial sector by allowing default risk to spread from the credit to the investment business. Universal banks that are affected by loan defaults may be forced to sell their security holdings. Large sales coupled with narrow markets may lead to accumulative effects which endanger the stability of the entire economy. The question of whether universal banks stabilize or destabilize the financial sector depends to a large extent on the risk correlation of their business lines. Risk-uncorrelated business lines enhance stability via risk diversification, whereas risk-correlated business lines expose a bank to risk accumulation. Thus universal banks have strong incentives to provide their credit and investment services within a wide variety of industries in order to compensate unexpected losses suffered in one business line by unexpected profits earned in another business line.

Focusing on a single industry, on the other hand, may be encouraged by information economies of specialization. Although these information economies are of major importance in many parts of the nonfinancial sector, they are usually outweighed by diversification advantages and are therefore of minor importance in the financial sector. Ordinary universal banks will try to provide their services to customers from a wide variety of industries. Under these circumstances the danger of risk accumulation is less severe.

Industry-specific financial distress, resulting, for example, from inter-industry competition, can be absorbed by diversified universal banks. Only economy-wide crises may lead to cumulative breakdowns in the banking sector. In this case, however, universal banks do not cause, but rather suffer from, the consequences of economic crises.[41]

Agency costs Ordinary universal banks enhance agency costs by weakening the market for corporate control. Since corporate takeovers threaten their information rents, ordinary universal banks will support incumbent management in its effort to fight off hostile takeovers. As a result, the market for corporate control, already suffering from the weakness of the entire investment sector, cannot produce strong disciplinary effects.

The governance activities of ordinary universal banks are focused on loan monitoring. Since ordinary universal banks are precluded from exercising non-default decision rights via equity ownership, proxy voting and board representation, they cannot reduce agency costs beyond the control of default risk.

Privileged universal banks

Basic features Unlike ordinary universal banks, privileged universal banks exercise control over non-banks through equity holdings, proxy rights and board representation. Hence, privileged universal banks are in an even stronger position to protect their information rents than are ordinary universal banks. Privileged universal banks can directly control their customers' financial decisions.

Domestic investment banks cannot successfully compete with privileged universal banks. Without strong competition from foreign (neoclassically regulated) investment banks, the entire financial system will be dominated by domestic privileged universal banks which try to earn information rents in the credit sector. Investment banking know-how will be lost. Capital market forces will be heavily impaired. Firms will depend on retained earnings and bank loans to finance their investments.

Knowledge utilization By weakening the investment banking sector, privileged universal banks impair the ability of capital markets to aggregate and transmit large amounts of scattered knowledge. Underdeveloped capital markets cannot attract a large number of investors. Even if the individual error terms of capital market participants are uncorrelated, the total number of investors will be too small to eliminate investment errors. Stock prices will not accurately signal investment opportunities.

On the other hand, privileged universal banks help their customers to overcome the problem of credit rationing, promote long-term investment perspectives, create useful knowledge links and reduce the costs of financial distress. Customers of privileged universal banks are able to escape credit rationing. Increasing interest rates do not automatically expose privileged universal banks to higher default risk. Unlike commercial and ordinary universal banks, privileged universal banks possess information about and control over their customers' default risk. Consequently, privileged universal banks are not confronted with the same information asymmetries and conflicts of interest as are commercial and ordinary universal banks.

Firms which are controlled by privileged universal banks through a combination of equity ownership, proxy voting and board representation are likely to be compensated for the impairment of capital markets by their banks' commitment to provide long-term finance for large investment projects. Commercial and ordinary universal banks will refuse to provide bank loans for most of these projects, because they fear to bear the high default risk of the early investment stages without benefiting from low default risk at later stages of successful projects. After these long-term investment projects prove successful, most firms will try to substitute bank loans by cheaper forms of capital. The combination of equity ownership and non-default decision rights assures privileged universal banks of benefiting from successful long-term investment projects.

Board representation by bank executives may establish useful knowledge links. Bank executives who serve on corporate boards acquire corporate and industry-specific insider knowledge. Although banks may acquire some of this knowledge through other channels, the tacit dimension of this knowledge can only be acquired through personal presence and involvement. It cannot be transmitted through regular communication channels. Tacit knowledge cannot be articulated. It is, at least to some extent, subconscious and has to be acquired in a learning-by-doing fashion. Tacit knowledge is embedded in its environment and can only be acquired via personal presence within this environment. Despite its importance, the tacit dimension of human knowledge has often been neglected. Tacit knowledge enables bank executives to more accurately predict economic trends and developments. Superior prediction of future events will result in turn in a better allocation of financial resources. In addition, personal knowledge links facilitate inter-firm exchange of embedded tacit knowledge and enhance coordination and cooperation among the involved firms and industries. Of course, the knowledge ties which are established through a network of board representation by bank executives will usually be of limited strength compared to closer forms of inter-firm cooperation such as production partnerships or joint ventures. Board representation by bank executives nevertheless improves bank performance and allocation of bank funds, as it enables banks to base their credit decisions on a more complete and more accurate knowledge set.

Based on the exercise of non-default decision rights, privileged universal banks can take preventive measures, and if necessary initiate corporate restructurings at an early stage of financial distress. The ability to intervene at an early stage of financial distress, coupled with access to insider knowledge and sophisticated effect information, enables privileged universal banks to reduce the costs associated with financial distress.

Risk diversification As has been discussed in connection with ordinary universal banks, universal banking does not cause adverse risk effects. Like ordinary universal banks, privileged universal banks will try to diversify their investments in order to withstand the effects of unexpected economic and financial developments.

Agency costs Privileged universal banks fill the governance vacuum created by ownership fragmentation and inactive markets for corporate control. By accumulating proxy voting rights, privileged universal banks exercise corporate governance on behalf of a large number of small investors without incurring nondiversification costs. Privileged universal banks, which have access to inside information and possess sophisticated effect knowledge, can detect corporate inefficiencies more effectively than ordinary shareholders. In addition, delegated corporate governance by privileged universal banks avoids unnecessary duplication of monitoring costs.

The accumulation of proxy voting rights may give privileged universal banks control over corporations in which they do not hold any shares. This creates opportunities for a bank to pursue its own interests at the expense of corporate shareholders. For example, privileged universal banks may transfer profits from corporations which they control via proxy voting rights to their own accounts by forcing these corporations to purchase overpriced bank services. However, privileged universal banks which do not restrict themselves with respect to this kind of bank opportunism will deprive themselves of future profits by ruining their reputation and impairing the competitiveness of their customers. Moreover, this kind of short-term opportunism is at least partly restricted by the transferability of proxy rights. Shareholders who are not satisfied with their bank's proxy voting possess strong incentives to transfer these rights to more reliable agents.

Holding companies

Basic features Holding companies issue shares in order to raise funds for the acquisition of major equity stakes in a limited number of firms. The intention to seize control over these firms distinguishes holding companies from investment companies and investment trusts. The main objective of investment companies and investment trusts is to diversify investment risk. This objective contrasts with holding large equity blocks of single firms. Holding companies, on the other hand, forego optional levels of risk diversification in exchange for corporate control.

Unlike multidivisional organizations, holding companies usually hold less than 100 percent of their subsidiaries' outstanding equity. Nor do holding companies provide their subsidiaries with a wide spectrum of support services. The holding company itself consists of a small team of managers. Each manager presides over or is a member of a subsidiary's board of directors. As board members, they monitor the activities of subsidiary firms. Besides monitoring subsidiaries, their main task is managing the holding company's portfolio. This activity includes the acquisition and sale of equity blocks and the reinvestment of dividend payments.

Holding companies do not employ internal control and information systems to coordinate the activities of their subsidiaries.[42] The ties to the holding company are limited to financial and personal relations. The subsidiary firms operate independently and separately. They neither use common corporate symbols nor do they transfer products or services amongst each other without using market interfaces. As a result, new subsidiaries can easily be integrated into the existing organizational structure.

Since holding companies usually own well below 100 percent of their subsidiaries, the subsidiaries remain listed on regular stock exchanges and significant amounts of each subsidiary's outstanding shares are traded on the stock market. Stock prices inform the holding company's management about the market value of each subsidiary.

Holding companies enhance ownership concentration through the process of pyramiding. Figure 1.4 explains the effect of pyramiding. The major shareholder in Figure 1.4 (a) owns 50 percent of the outstanding shares of corporation A whose equity totals 10 million. As shown in Figure 1.4 (b), instead of directly investing in corporation A, the same shareholder could buy 50 percent of the outstanding shares of a holding company which in turn invests its equity of 10 million in 50 percent holdings of corporation A and corporation B, whose equity also totals 10 million. In this simple example, pyramiding allows the major shareholder to double his or her equity control. The pyramiding effect can be multiplied by creating intermediate holding companies.

Knowledge utilization Majority ownership and capital market information enable holding companies to base their investment decisions on insider and scattered knowledge. As majority shareholders, holding companies have privileged access to inside

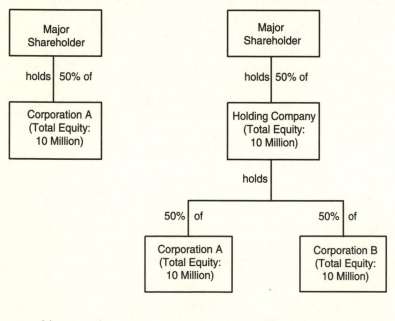

(a)   (b)

Figure 1.4 Ownership concentration through pyramiding

information about their subsidiaries' economic and financial performance. Personal ties guarantee that the information transfer is not limited to the explicit dimension of investment-relevant information, but also includes tacit knowledge. Their subsidiaries' stock prices provide holding companies with scattered knowledge. Since the management team of a holding company consists of experienced, well-trained and highly skilled investment experts, holding companies combine their insider and scattered knowledge with highly sophisticated effect information.

As a result of closer personal ties and more concentrated ownership, holding companies usually acquire larger amounts of firm-specific insider knowledge than do investment companies or investment trusts. Compared to multidivisional organizations, on the other hand, holding companies possess less insider knowledge, because divisions within a multidivisional organization are usually more inclusively monitored than subsidiaries within a holding company.

Risk diversification Pyramiding effects enable large investors to diversify unsystematic investment risk without sacrificing majority control. Nevertheless, risk diversification within holding companies remains incomplete. Holding companies which obtain majority ownership and exercise control over their subsidiaries do not achieve the same level of risk diversification as investment companies and investment trusts.

Agency costs Holding companies possess strong incentives to monitor their subsidiaries. As majority owners, they earn positive returns from their governance activities. Since holding companies usually do not own 100 percent of their subsidiaries' outstanding capital, small shareholders will benefit from the governance activities of holding companies. In exchange, holding companies obtain cost-free price information about the capital market's perception of their subsidiaries' economic and financial perspectives. Trying to internalize all governance benefits would sacrifice these information advantages.

The information which is aggregated and transmitted by stock prices not only improves capital allocation, but also contributes to the reduction of agency costs by providing objective measures for evaluating the performance of subsidiary firms. While multidivisional organizations rely exclusively on internal accounting data when assessing the performance of division managers, holding companies have recourse to more objective capital market measures

71

when assessing the management of subsidiaries. Furthermore, regular stock price information facilitates implementation of the shareholder value concept.[43] According to this concept, every management decision should be evaluated by its impact on the firm's market value. Unlike division managers, chief executives of subsidiary firms can be directly compensated on the basis of the firm's market value as determined by stock market capitalization. In addition, holding companies may use stock options as part of an incentive-oriented compensation plan for major executives of subsidiary firms. These performance-based control instruments facilitate corporate governance at the subsidiary level.

Low agency costs at the subsidiary level are a necessary but not sufficient condition for monitoring efficiency within holding companies. Low agency costs at the subsidiary level may be offset by major inefficiencies at the holding company level. Shareholders of the holding company are confronted with exactly the same kind of agency problems as the holding company itself has to deal with as shareholder of its subsidiaries. Hence, the same conditions which resulted in monitoring efficiency at the subsidiary level will also limit agency problems efficiently at the holding company level. These conditions include ownership concentration and the availability of regular stock quotations. Ownership concentration guarantees an efficient level of monitoring activities. Regular stock quotations facilitate performance evaluation.

If ownership at the holding company level is highly fragmented, corporate governance relies exclusively on capital market forces. Small shareholders cannot earn positive returns from their governance activities. Exit is the efficient way to express their dissatisfaction. Unlike investors of mutual funds, however, minor shareholders of holding companies cannot discipline management by redeeming their shares. Like investors of closed-end funds, they have to sell their shares in secondary capital markets. Dissatisfied shareholders who sell their stocks will cause a decline in the holding company's market value, which in turn will increase the probability of an unfriendly takeover and will impair the holding company's ability to raise new funds.

Multidivisional organization

Basic features Multidivisional organizations consist of a general office, centralized units and operating divisions (see Figure 1.5).

Unlike functional units, divisions are created along product lines or market sectors. Each division may be regarded as a unitary firm which is divided along functional lines. Although all divisions, in general, are commonly owned and use the same corporate name and symbols, they operate rather independently. The general office refrains from involving itself in daily routines. All operating divisions are delegated to the divisional level.

The general office is responsible for monitoring divisional performance. Since all divisions are usually 100 percent subsidiaries, the general office has no recourse to capital market information. The investment relationship between the general office and divisions is completely internalized. Both general office and divisions act under

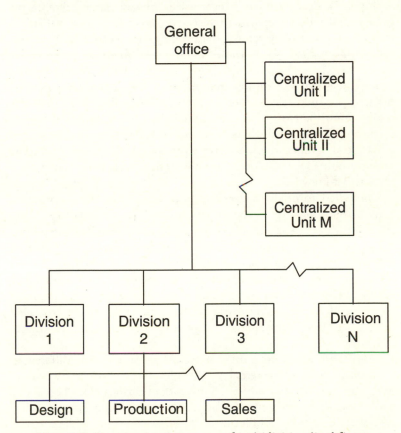

Figure 1.5 Organizational structure of multidivisionalized firms

common ownership. Their relationship is coordinated by internal incentive, information and control systems.

Cash flows are not automatically reinvested at their sources, but allocated to high-yield uses by the general office without incurring the costs of bank intermediation or capital market imperfections. Because the coordination and allocation functions are performed by the general office, multidivisionalized firms are often characterized as internal or miniature capital markets.[44]

Knowledge utilization Multidivisional organizations combine sophisticated effect knowledge with an unlimited access to inside information. The management team at the general office consists of highly skilled investment experts who possess large amounts of general and industry-specific investment experience. Internal information and control systems provide the general office with timely inside information about the economic and financial situation of each division. Since capital allocation within multidivisional organizations does not use capital market interfaces, insider regulations cannot preclude the general office from allocating financial resources on the basis of insider knowledge. By eliminating capital market interfaces, multidivisional organizations sacrifice the ability to base capital allocation on scattered knowledge. Capital allocation within multidivisional organizations relies exclusively on public and insider knowledge.

Compared to other modes of capital allocation, multidivisional organization enjoys by far the largest comparative information advantages in those cases where capital allocation among competing divisions requires large amounts of insider knowledge. Superior effect information may enable the general office of a multidivisional organization to realize minor advantages whenever capital resources have to be allocated on the basis of public knowledge, whereas the relevance of scattered knowledge will put multidivisional organizations at a clear disadvantage compared to other forms of capital allocation.

Immediate access to a division's cash flow, and cost differences between internal and external communication, constitute two additional advantages of multidivisional organizations. Unlike capital market investors, the general office of a multidivisional organization possesses the ability to allocate cash flows to high-yield uses in a real-time fashion. Within multidivisional organizations, cash flows are not automatically reinvested at their source, but instead allocated to their most promising use by the visible hand of the general office. The invisible hand of unintermediated capital markets, on the other hand, is limited to allocating only those portions of a firm's cash flow which are paid out to shareholders in the form of quarterly or yearly dividends and share repurchases. Thus, unlike the general office of a multidivisional organization, the invisible hand of capital markets has no immediate access to a firm's cash flow. Moreover, executives of freestanding firms may withhold large amounts of cash flows from capital market allocation by accumulating hidden reserves.

Multidivisional organization benefits from the advantages of internal communication. Informing the general office of the expected return and risk of alternative investment proposals at divisional level incurs less communication costs than conveying the same amount of information to a large number of anonymous capital market investors. In addition, multidivisional organizations are able to overcome the problems associated with incomplete information and the resulting investment uncertainty. As Williamson and Bhargava (1972: 137–8) point out, multidivisional organizations decompose uncertain investment projects into several stages and reevaluate their investment decisions from stage to stage. Efforts to design equivalent contractual arrangements at capital market interfaces will fail because of prohibitively high evaluation and enforcement costs.

Risk diversification The multidivisional structure facilitates corporate growth and diversification.[45] Newly acquired firms can easily be integrated into the existing divisional structure without undergoing major reorganization. Since each division operates somewhat independently, multidivisional organizations may integrate firms from different industries into the multidivisional structure in order to diversify unsystematic investment risk. Nevertheless, multidivisional organizations are usually less diversified than investment companies and investment trusts. Multidivisional organizations trade off risk diversification in favor of insider knowledge and lower agency costs at the divisional level.

Agency costs Multidivisional organization creates strong incentives to monitor division managers. 100 percent ownership of divisions perfectly internalizes all monitoring benefits. Based on industry experience and internal accounting data, managers at the general office can easily discern to what extent division managers may be held responsible for the performance of their division and to what extent divisional performance may be attributed to uncontrollable environmental factors. Ordinary capital market investors, on the other hand, would have to incur prohibitively high information costs in order to accurately evaluate managerial performance within freestanding firms.

The ability of the general office to assess managerial decision processes in its entirety enhances risk-neutral decision making by division managers (see Williamson and Bhargava 1972: 136). Executives of freestanding firms, on the other hand, will act risk-averse whenever outcomes instead of decision-situations are the basis of performance evaluation.

While division managers who do not possess the required management skills or try to pursue their own interests at the expense of the company's economic and financial success will be immediately replaced by the general office, substituting incumbent managers of freestanding firms imposes (sometimes prohibitively) high costs on dissatisfied shareholders. They must either convince fellow shareholders of the necessity to replace incumbent managers, or acquire a majority of shares through a successful takeover bid. Convincing fellow shareholders may fail as a result of information asymmetries. Poison pills, greenmail, golden parachutes and other anti-takeover measures may prevent corporate takeovers.

While praising the governance advantages of an internal incentive, information and control apparatus, proponents of the multidivisional structure tend to ignore the problem of monitoring the general office. Unlike mutual funds, multidivisional organizations do not allow their shareholders to discipline management by redeeming shares. Shareholders of multidivisional organizations find themselves in a similar position as shareholders of holding companies or investors of closed-end funds. In the absence of major shareholders, managers at the general office will be encouraged to pursue their own goals rather than maximizing shareholder wealth.

Under dispersed ownership, the reduction of agency costs at the general office level relies exclusively on capital market forces. Minor shareholders cannot internalize sufficiently large parts of monitoring benefits in order to cover monitoring costs. They will prefer to sell their shares if investment returns do not meet their expectations. Cumulative sales will result in declining share prices. Without the disciplinary effects of an active market for corporate control, however, capital market forces will remain ineffective. Unless potential takeovers put their human capital in jeopardy, managers at the general office will enjoy wide discretionary freedoms. On-the-job consumption in form of mahogany desks, pretty but less qualified secretaries or firm-owned yachts are some potential consequences. Another is the expansion of multidivisional organizations into unprofitable conglomerates. In their quest for more power and risk diversification, managers at the general office will favor the acquisition of new firms instead of paying out cash flows as dividends, even if these new acquisitions reduce shareholder wealth.

As multidivisional organizations grow, managers at the general office will become further emancipated from the disciplinary forces of capital markets. It becomes increasingly difficult for potential bidders to acquire the necessary financial resources in order to submit successful takeover bids.

Leveraged buyout associations

Basic features The organizational and financial structure of leveraged buyout associations is shown in Figure 1.6. Although at first glance the structure of an LBO association does not differ substantially from the basic structure of a multidivisional organization, major differences prevail. LBO associations are run by limited partnerships. Unlike general offices within multidivisional organizations, LBO partners provide only a very limited amount of management and governance services. Their main task is to plan and realize new buyouts. The partners do not possess the necessary industry experience and management skills to effectively manage and monitor each buyout firm. The activities of LBO partners are focused on the identification of target firms and the acquisition of financial resources.

Leveraged buyouts are financed primarily by debt. The debt-equity ratio usually exceeds 5.5. Equity is provided by the buyout fund and the top executives of each LBO firm. Despite the high debt-equity ratio, top managers of each LBO firm hold substantial equity stakes. As a result, the pay-to-performance sensitivity of LBO executives is significantly higher than the pay-to-performance sensitivity of division managers or even chief executive officers of multidivisional organizations.[46]

Unlike divisions, LBO units have the legal status of independent

77

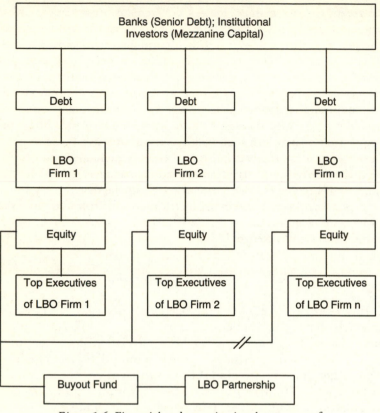

Figure 1.6 Financial and organizational structure of
LBO associations

corporations. This precludes LBO partners from transferring profits
across units for purposes of risk diversification or internal capital
allocation. All cash payouts go directly to the buyout fund, which is
usually organized as a limited partnership or closed-end fund.

A typical LBO process starts with the identification of a target
firm. For an LBO to be successful, target firms must have substantial
cash flow prospects. These cash flow prospects may stem from a
variety of sources: deductible tax obligations, corporate restructuring, asset sales, reduction of overhead and labor costs, operational
improvements, etc.

While less-known LBO partnerships have to search for target
firms, highly reputed LBO associations are often approached by a
target firm's incumbent managers with the request to assist in a

management buyout. Together with the management team which is supposed to run the target firm after the buyout, LBO partners develop a buyout strategy and project the target firm's future cash flow. The buyout strategy usually includes a drastic reduction in workforce, concentration of major decision rights within the hands of a small management team, divestiture of single assets or even entire divisions which do not belong to the firm's core business, reorganization of work and decision processes and other forms of corporate restructuring. If the projected cash flow is large enough to meet all financial obligations and promises to generate high profits, the LBO partners will try to raise the financial resources which are necessary to buy out the target firm.

If a target firm is highly diversified and has accumulated large inventories of unspecific assets, i.e. assets which are unrelated to the firm's core business, banks will agree to provide senior debt of up to 50–70 percent of the total buyout volume. However, banks will insist on floating interest rates in order to protect themselves against unexpected increases in interest rates.[47] Mezzanine capital provides another 20–30 percent of the buyout price. Being subordinated to senior debt, mezzanine capital can be characterized as high-risk debt. Although mezzanine capital is senior to equity, the chances are very low that suppliers of mezzanine capital will receive any repayments if the LBO firm is forced to enter bankruptcy. In exchange for bearing this high default risk, suppliers of mezzanine capital receive higher interest rate payments than suppliers of senior debt. Mezzanine capital provides a very lucrative investment for institutional investors such as investment companies, pension funds or insurance companies, who possess the financial resources to diversify high default risk. With the introduction of junk bond markets, mezzanine capital became even more attractive. The ability to trade mezzanine claims provided investors with high liquidity. As a result, private investors began entering the market and LBO partnerships had little trouble in acquiring sufficient financial resources.

After receiving the commitment of potential creditors to fund the buyout, the LBO partners will submit a takeover bid. The bidding stage is the most critical element of the LBO process. The takeover bid attracts competitive bidders who believe that the original bid is underpriced. Competitive bidding, especially by newcomers, will result in a winner's curse. Bidders are more likely to win if their bid is overpriced. Newly founded LBO partnerships have not yet built up reputational capital which they might lose as a result of a post-buyout bankruptcy. In the case of a successful buyout, on the other hand, unreputed LBO partnerships have much more to gain than LBO partnerships which already possess reputational capital. The combination of higher potential benefits in the case of successful buyouts and lower potential costs in case of unsuccessful buyouts encourages unreputed LBO partnerships to overprice their bids.

Subsequent to an accepted bid, the newly formed LBO firm will be stripped of all assets and divisions which are unrelated to the firm's core business. Highly diversified target firms are often transformed into several independent LBO firms. Former divisions of multidivisional organizations are restructured as independent LBO firms. Division managers become chief executives; general offices and centralized units disappear.

LBO organizations are not a permanent form of capital allocation and corporate governance. After a period of three to five years, the LBO partnership usually sells its equity stake to the public. By this time most LBO firms have regained their competitiveness and profitability. Through the sale, the LBO partnership will realize considerable capital gains in exchange for its restructuring activities.

Knowledge utilization   From the viewpoint of capital allocation, LBO associations repurchase outstanding shares, usually at high premiums. Although debt is issued in order to finance these repurchases, the basic source of all share redemptions is the firm's post-buyout cash flow. Most of the buyout debt is scheduled to be repaid within the first year after the buyout. The conventional process of capital allocation is literally reversed. Instead of providing financial resources for the acquisition of physical and human capital, corporate assets are reallocated to more effective uses in exchange for financial resources. These financial resources are then repaid to shareholders, who originally provided financial resources for the acquisition of physical and human capital. At the same time, the process of ownership fragmentation is reversed. Dispersed ownership rights are reconcentrated within the hands of corporate managers and LBO partners.

Risk diversification   Leveraged buyouts are not motivated by diversification considerations. By breaking up large conglomerates, LBO associations reverse the process of risk diversification. A diversified conglomerate is transformed into several undiversified firms. Despite the break-up of diversified conglomerates, LBO partners do not have to bear high levels of undiversified risk. The portfolio of the LBO fund is usually well diversified because the LBO partnership holds equity stakes in a large number of LBO firms.

Unlike LBO partners, managers of LBO firms have to bear high levels of undiversified risk. In addition to their human capital, managers of LBO firms invest large amounts of financial resources in their LBO firms. As mentioned above, managers of LBO firms usually acquire large equity positions in their firms.

Agency costs The financial structure of LBO firms minimizes agency costs. Managers and LBO partners hold large equity stakes in LBO firms. Since their own wealth is immediately affected by their management decisions, they possess strong incentives to eliminate inefficiencies. Yet the strongest disciplinary effect results from high-leveraged debt financing. The high debt burden pushes each buyout firm toward the edge of bankruptcy and leaves little room for on-the-job consumption and other forms of managerialism. LBO managers, who have their human capital and large equity holdings at stake, are exposed to an exceptionally strong performance pressure. They must generate high cash flows in order to meet all debt obligations. Even if an LBO firm is highly profitable, interest and principal payments will extract most of the free cash flow. LBO managers cannot dispose over-large amounts of free cash flow like many corporate managers. In particular, LBO managers cannot withhold interest and principal payments from creditors in the same way as managers of publicly held corporations often withhold dividend payments from small shareholders. If LBO managers fail to meet all debt requirements, their firm will be forced into bankruptcy.

Although most leveraged buyouts result in high efficiency gains,[48] the largest governance benefit stems from those leveraged buyouts which are never realized, but present a continuous threat of occurring as soon as corporate managers fail to maximize shareholder value. The high profits associated with successful leveraged buyouts encourage economic actors to screen publicly held corporations. High-leveraged debt financing enables LBO partners to raise enormous amounts of capital, making even the largest publicly held corporations potential buyout targets. As a result, managers of holding companies and multidivisional conglomerates are exposed to buyout threats if they fail to maximize shareholder wealth.

Financial keiretsu

Basic features Financial keiretsu consist of about twenty to fifty firms which form a network of cross shareholdings, directorship interlockings, debt funding, product trading and informal communication. Despite their legal independence, most of the membership firms share common names and logos to signal their keiretsu affiliation. All membership firms usually operate in different industries or at least different market segments. As a consequence, membership firms seldom compete directly with each other. Although each individual company, including financial institutions, owns only a minor fraction (< 5 percent) of another member firm's equity base, aggregate ownership of all members is typically large enough (20–30 percent) to ensure substantial group control and insulate membership firms from takeover raids.

The financial core of a keiretsu organization is composed of a city bank, a trust bank, a life-insurance company and a large trading company. These financial institutions do not only hold the largest equity shares among keiretsu firms; they also represent the most important sources of debt funding for membership firms. The major debt relationships within the financial core and between the financial core and nonfinancial keiretsu firms are schematized in Figure 1.7.

The most dominant financial position within each keiretsu is held by a city bank. City banks are large commercial banks which are entitled to hold limited equity stakes in non-banks. Of outstanding importance is the city bank's role as main bank for many keiretsu firms as well as for the keiretsu's trading company. The main bank relationship consists of close financial, personal and informational ties. Although keiretsu firms borrow from a variety of affiliated and unaffiliated financial institutions, the main bank is the primary lender of short-term debt. Keiretsu firms rely to a large extent on this short-term debt to finance long-term investment projects. So these short-term credits have to be rolled over continuously.[49] The economic rationale behind this maturity mismatch is twofold. First, it provides the main bank with more accurate information about its customers' financial situation.[50] This information originates from two sources: the way in which the firm fulfills its regular debt obligations and the financial data it discloses when asking for credit to be rolled over. Second, the maturity mismatch creates a legal basis for the main bank to claim a troubled firm's decision rights at an early stage of financial distress. Since the

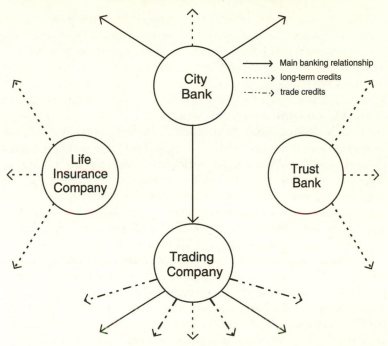

Figure 1.7 Major debt relationships within the financial core and between the financial core and nonfinancial keiretsu firms

maturity mismatch leads to a strong main bank dependency among keiretsu firms, it may also be interpreted as a bondage to ensure inter-keiretsu cooperation.

Information asymmetries between the main bank and keiretsu firms are further reduced by daily bank account information and close involvement of bank executives in all major investment and management decisions. In addition to consulting the main bank when developing major business strategies, keiretsu firms regularly provide their main bank with internal accounting data and performance reports. Most of this information exchange is institutionalized by director interlinkages and through membership in the presidents' club (Sheard 1989a: 403). In the presidents' club, chief executives of all major keiretsu firms meet regularly to discuss important economic developments. Although these meetings have a rather informal character, their importance as a regular knowledge link should not be understated.

The second most important financial institution within a keiretsu network is a large trading company. Besides intermediating product markets and helping keiretsu firms to enter new, especially foreign markets, trading companies perform important banking and insurance functions within a financial keiretsu. As shown in Figure 1.7, the trading company serves as the main bank for many keiretsu firms. In addition, the trading company provides keiretsu firms with trade credits. Apart from their financial impact, these trade credits enhance inter-firm risk-sharing within the financial keiretsu (Sheard 1989b). Without the financial services of a trading company, firms who want to insure their trade credits against default risk would have to purchase the services of insurance companies. By pooling uncorrelated default risk, insurance companies could level out revenue variations and enable participating firms to share individual risk. However, insurance companies who insure trade credits will be confronted with adverse selection and moral hazard problems. As long as the insurance company is an outsider to the insured transactions, it has to incur high costs of verifying individual default risk. Moreover, an outside insurance company can hardly control the credit risk to which suppliers expose themselves after they have contracted insurance services. A trading company, which is directly involved in the trading process and has access to additional inside information via its main bank relationship to most trading parties, is not exposed to the same adverse selection and moral hazard problems as an outside insurance company, and therefore can provide insurance services at considerably lower costs.

As the trading company's main bank, the keiretsu's city bank exercises substantial control over the trading company. Prior to each major business decision, the trading company is expected to obtain approval by the keiretsu's city bank. According to Bronte (1982: 117) the roll-over loans provided by city banks to trading companies "have evolved into what is essentially preferred stock in their trading company clients, and the interest payments are regarded more as semi-annual dividends."

While city banks and trading companies rely heavily on short-term finance, mainly deposits (city banks) and short-term loans (trading companies), trust banks and life insurance companies receive the majority of their funds from more reliable and less expensive long-term financial commitments. The major liabilities of trust banks are trust accounts and private pension funds. Life insurance companies, of course, are funded primarily through life insurance policies. Trust banks and life insurance companies provide fellow keiretsu firms with long-term debt. In addition, life insurance companies have evolved as one of the keiretsu's major shareholders. In exchange for their debt and equity investments, life insurance companies receive most of the keiretsu's life insurance business.[51]

Life insurance firms which belong to a financial keiretsu network are organized as mutual companies. Contrary to trading companies, trust banks and life insurance mutuals are not exposed to direct main bank monitoring, nor do they themselves exercise control over their customers on the basis of debt maturity mismatches.[52] Agency costs are instead contained by the awareness of mutual dependency, cross shareholdings, federal regulation and low levels of information asymmetries.

Another important element of keiretsu organizations is their strong commitment to lifetime employment. Employees as well as managers enjoy a high degree of job security. Even those managers who have been replaced by rescue teams during a period of financial distress are often reinstalled in their former positions after the process of corporate restructuring has been successfully completed. The lifetime employment relationship encourages employees, executives, and managers to invest in keiretsu- and firm-specific human capital.

In general, specific investments are fostered throughout the keiretsu network by inter-firm risk-sharing and the prevailing governance structure. Specific investments lead to an increase in firm-specific risk. However, keiretsu firms smoothen their individual profit variations by the risk-sharing effect of cross shareholdings. Inter-firm dividend payments will decrease the gap between highly profitable and less profitable firms.[53] Furthermore, a firm which invests in keiretsu-specific assets is assured by the prevailing governance structure that fellow keiretsu members will not attempt to appropriate the resulting dependency in order to generate short-term profits. On the contrary, keiretsu-specific investments by a member firm induce fellow companies to invest in co-specific assets, thus creating even higher levels of mutual dependency. Consequently, decision makers have strong incentives to include potential effects of their investment decisions on fellow keiretsu firms into their calculations. Moreover, decision makers who fail to maximize overall keiretsu wealth face severe disciplinary measures, mainly executed by city banks or trading companies.

Knowledge utilization   Financial keiretsu utilize a wide variety of knowledge during the process of capital allocation, eliminate the problem of credit rationing, encourage long-term investments into specific assets and reduce the cost of financial distress. The informational and personal linkages within the keiretsu supply the financial core with a wide range of inside information. Trade credits, short-term loans which are continuously rolled over and regular bank accounts provide city banks and trading companies with inside information about the economic and financial perspective of fellow keiretsu firms. Director interlinkages and regular meetings of chief executives (presidents' club) facilitate the transmission of tacit knowledge.

The financial core's access to inside information is not limited to the production stages of single firms, but usually encompasses the entire value chain, including suppliers and customers. Due to the wide spectrum of sources for inside information, keiretsu organizations realize synergy effects with respect to incomplete information. Fragmentary knowledge which would be worthless to most organizations becomes highly valuable in combination with complementary knowledge fragments from other information sources within financial keiretsu. The financial core's sophisticated effect knowledge further enhances these information synergies. As a result, financial keiretsu are able to base investment decisions on the same level of insider knowledge as holding companies, although the financial core of a keiretsu network does not exercise majority control over fellow keiretsu firms.

The absence of internal information and control systems, on the other hand, prevents financial keiretsu from generating the same level of insider knowledge as multidivisional organizations. Unlike multidivisonal organizations, however, financial keiretsu do not supplant capital market forces. Substantial amounts of each keiretsu firm's outstanding shares are regularly traded on stock exchanges, enabling market forces to aggregate and transmit considerable amounts of scattered knowledge. Again, strong similarities to holding companies prevail.

Contrary to multidivisional organizations and holding companies, capital allocation within financial keiretsu is primarily based on debt. As a result of low information asymmetries and effective governance structures, the problem of credit rationing does not exist within financial keiretsu, despite the fact that the financial core supplies only a part of each member firm's total debt. As noted above, the remaining part is provided by financial institutions not belonging to the keiretsu network. Consequently, one might expect that outside borrowing from a plurality of sources will increase a keiretsu firm's cost of debt due to multiplication of screening and monitoring expenditures by outside lenders. However, non-keiretsu lenders do not have to incur screening and monitoring costs, but benefit from the main bank's commitment to enter a long-term relationship with fellow keiretsu firms. Although the main bank is not the exclusive lender of keiretsu members, long-term relationship and mutual dependency create a strong incentive to invest in screening and monitoring activities. Access to inside information and keiretsu-specific enforcement mechanisms enables the main bank to screen and monitor investment projects more effectively and at considerably lower costs than outside lenders. As a result of the long-term relationship with a keiretsu affiliate, screening and monitoring is not only less expensive, but also more valuable for main banks. The information which is acquired through screening and monitoring generates insider knowledge about the firm's current financial situation and future economic perspectives.

A bank's commitment to enter a long-term main bank relationship with fellow keiretsu firms credibly signals the bank's intention to invest in screening and monitoring and limit the danger of bankruptcy. Even in the case of bankruptcy, outside lenders can rely on the main bank's incentive to prevent losses in reputation capital by granting seniority rights to outside lenders and bearing the majority of the default costs. A main bank which fails to minimize bankruptcy costs for outside investors would lose its reputation as a reliable "delegated monitor," thereby increasing the entire keiretsu's cost of debt. Outside lenders would either completely refrain from lending to the main bank's customers, or charge higher interest rates to cover their screening and monitoring expenditures. If the main bank, on the other hand, effectively screens and monitors fellow keiretsu firms, outside lenders will benefit from free-riding on the main bank's activities. Competitive forces will compel outside lenders to share these benefits with borrowing firms, which in turn will reward main banks for their role as "delegated monitor" by offering favorable exchange fees, compensating balances and similar privileges (see Horiuchi 1989: 266).

Since the existence of a main bank relationship reduces the default risk for outside lenders, keiretsu firms are able to acquire larger amounts of debt to finance specific investments than are independent firms. Remember that specific investments have a relatively high value as long as the firm remains solvent, but lose much of their value in case of bankruptcy. Consequently, specific investments expose creditors to a higher default risk than unspecific investments whose value does not depend upon a firm's solvency.

Despite the main bank's commitment, outside borrowing by keiretsu firms is limited. The main bank which has its reputation, equity and its own loans at risk will use its authority to keep outside leverage at reasonable levels. Moreover, outside lenders will be reluctant to expose themselves to excessive default risk, because as creditors they are not rewarded with higher profit expectations in exchange for bearing extra risk.

Unlike outside lenders, main banks have an incentive to fund risky projects of keiretsu members. The main bank relationship allows for the adjustment of short-term interest rates to firm-specific risk. Since the main bank bears large portions of a fellow keiretsu firm's investment risk, the interest payments are often adjusted in a dividend-like manner. Profit-correlated interest payments encourage main banks to provide keiretsu members with short-term debt for risky investment projects which would otherwise be subject to credit rationing. In fact the main bank relationship creates what might be called hybrid finance or "dequity"—a combination of the disciplinary forces of debt and the residual claims associated with equity. Compared to debt, dequity solves the problem of credit rationing. Compared to equity, it reduces the agency costs of free cash flow and prevents the negative signaling effects which are associated with equity issues.

The wide variety of lenders, ranging from outside lenders to main banks, trading companies, trust banks and life insurance companies, not only reduces individual loan risk, but also results in a debt structure which is well suited to the individual situation of each keiretsu firm. Except for outside lenders, all creditors are engaged in a long-term relationship with borrowing keiretsu firms. As a result, long-term investments will be more favorably evaluated within keiretsu networks than within other forms of capital allocation and corporate governance. Capital-market-based modes especially tend to overdiscount future returns as a consequence of the prevailing information asymmetries and uncertainties.

Based on the maturity mismatch between short-term credits and long-term investments, the main bank is able to intervene at an early stage of a keiretsu firm's financial distress. As soon as a keiretsu firm is expected to encounter financial problems, bank representatives will meet with the firm's management in order to develop preventive strategies. If the firm's management team does not possess the necessary skills to effectively restructure the company, the main bank will temporarily install a specialized rescue team. With the consent and help of fellow keiretsu members, troubled firms are able to survive even under situations of extreme financial distress. By extending its own credits, providing interest subsidies, guaranteeing loan repayment or even injecting new equity, the main bank signals the keiretsu's commitment to prevent a troubled firm from entering bankruptcy. These signals usually encourage outside lenders to refrain from withdrawing credits and demanding bankruptcy proceedings.

Despite the absence of an active market for control of keiretsu firms, financial keiretsu enjoy a high degree of adaptability. Corporate restructuring is usually enforced by the main bank, which has up-to-date insider knowledge about each keiretsu firm's economic perspective. As noted, this knowledge is generated through information from a wide variety of sources such as the presidents' club, trade credits, short-term loans, director interlinkages, upstream suppliers, downstream customers and stock prices. Nevertheless, one caveat remains. When a keiretsu firm enters bankruptcy, the reputation of its main bank will be severely damaged. Another asset to be lost in the course of a keiretsu firm's bankruptcy will be the firm-specific insider knowledge which the main bank has acquired during its close relationship with the troubled firm. To protect their intangible assets, main banks will invest more resources in an affiliate's rescue than other banks. As a result, non-viable firms will be kept alive longer than they should be (see Horiuchi 1989: 269).

Risk diversification Financial keiretsu succeed in generating large amounts of insider knowledge without incurring high non-diversification costs. Investment risk is well diversified within financial keiretsu. Cross shareholdings diversify unsystematic investment risks. Since financial keiretsu usually consist of no more than one firm per industry, firm-specific investment risks is highly uncorrelated.

Credit risk is shared by a large number of lenders including the financial core and outside creditors. Of course, the main bank practically insures outside creditors against default risk. But since the main bank plays the role of an outside creditor by lending to firms which belong to other keiretsu networks, it benefits from the default insurance provided by city banks and trading companies of other keiretsu networks. As a result of this "system" of mutual insurance, overall credit risk is minimized.

Agency costs   Agency costs are effectively reduced within financial keiretsu through a combination of incentive alignment, main bank monitoring and reciprocal governance. Financial keiretsu mitigate agency problems through lifetime employment and profit-based salary bonuses. The commitment to lifetime employment creates a high level of loyalty among keiretsu employees and executives at all levels. As a result of their lifetime employment, executives of keiretsu firms will discount future effects of current activities on the keiretsu's competitiveness at relatively low rates. Since all employees and executives of keiretsu firms receive a large portion of their regular salary and future retirement benefits in form of profit-based bonuses, their income is immediately affected by their firm's competitiveness. The resulting team spirit and mutual dependency leaves little room for on-the-job consumption and other forms of opportunism.

In addition, each member firm's management is continuously monitored by main bank executives. The main bank does not only bear the entire default risk of fellow keiretsu firms. It also participates in the firm's profit through equity ownership and adjustable interest rates ("dequity"). As a result, the main bank is able to internalize a large portion of the monitoring benefits, and thus possesses strong incentives to invest into monitoring activities.

Based on the maturity mismatch of short-term bank loans and long-term investment projects, the main bank can effectively monitor and discipline the management teams of fellow keiretsu firms. Moreover, the main bank has access to a wide spectrum of information channels in order to obtain performance-relevant information. These information channels include director interlinkages, informal meetings at the presidents' club, bank accounts, trade credits and equity ownership, as well as inter-keiretsu suppliers and customers. Even if a keiretsu firm's management does not provide main bank executives voluntarily with performance-relevant information, the main bank has little trouble in acquiring the necessary information.

Within financial keiretsu, the problem of "who monitors the monitor?," in this case "who monitors the financial core?" and in particular "who monitors the city bank?," is solved by reciprocal governance. Within each financial keiretsu, firms are closely monitored by their main bank, which is either the keiretsu's trading company or city bank. The trading company is monitored by the city bank, the trading company's main bank. Only the city bank, the trust bank and the life insurance bank do not have a main bank which monitors their activities. But this does not mean that managerial discretion remains unrestricted within these companies. Contrary to multidivisional organizations and holding companies, corporate governance within financial keiretsu is not structured hierarchically, but reciprocally. While neither divisions nor subsidiaries are able to exercise significant control over their respective headquarters, keiretsu members as a group own substantial amounts of the city bank's, trust bank's and life insurance company's outstanding shares. Based on the voting rights associated with these shares, keiretsu members as a group are able to initiate the replacement of inefficient management at all three companies.

Other forms

In addition to the organizational forms which have been discussed so far, insurance companies and pension funds might be considered as organizational responses to capital market inefficiencies. However, the distinguishing characteristics of insurance companies and pension funds are associated with their insurance and pension services, not their investment activities. As investors, insurance companies and pension funds act like other institutional investors: they invest large amounts of capital and are subjected to specific regulations. Nevertheless, they do not represent unique modes of capital organization and corporate governance, and are therefore treated as institutional investors and not as organizational responses to capital market inefficiencies.

Summary

Figure 1.8 summarizes the relevant characteristics of neoclassical capital markets, relational capital markets, investment companies and investment trusts, commercial banks, investment banks, ordinary universal banks, privileged universal banks, holding companies, multidivisional organizations, leveraged buyout associations and financial keiretsu as alternative modes of capital allocation and corporate governance.

	Capital allocation				Corporate governance	
	Use of scattered knowledge	Use of insider knowledge	Use of effect knowledge	Use of tacit knowledge/ knowledge links	Risk diversification	Reduction of agency costs
Unintermediated capital markets (neoclassical)	+ +	-	-	-	+	-
Unintermediated capital markets (relational)	+	+	+	-	+	+ +
Investment companies and investment trusts (neoclassical regulation)	+ +	+ *	+	-	+ +	+
Investment companies and investment trusts (relational regulation)	+	+ +	+ +	-	+ +	+
Commercial banks (neoclassical regulation)	-	+	+ +	-	+	+
Investment banks (neoclassical regulation)	-	-	+	-	+	+
Ordinary universal banks	+	+	+ +	-	+	+
Privileged universal banks	-	+ +	+ +	+ +	+	+
Holding companies	-	+ +	+ +	+	+	+ +
Multidivisional organizations	+	+ +	+ +	+	+	+ +
LBOs	-	+	+ +	-	+	+ +
Financial keiretsu	+	+ +	+ +	+ +	+ +	+ +

Figure 1.8 Comparative features of alternative modes of capital allocation and corporate governance

*	limited to fragmentary and unspecific insider knowledge
+ +	effective
+	partly effective
-	ineffective

DISCRIMINATING MATCH

The basic theoretical framework which has been developed so far suggests that the total amount of investment relation costs (IRC) of a given investment relation i depends upon the prevailing regulatory environment (RE_i), the relevant dimensions (D_{ij}) of the investment relation, and the organizational mode (OM_i) of capital allocation and corporate governance which is employed:

$$IRCi = f(REi; Dij; OMi) \text{ for all } i \qquad (1.5)$$

Since the level of industry maturity (IM) and the degree of investment plasticity (IP) have been identified as the relevant dimensions of an investment relation, equation (1.5) may be transformed into:

$$IRC_i = f(RE_i; IM_i; IP_i; OM_i) \text{ for all } i \qquad (1.5')$$

At the business level, the regulatory environment (RE) has to be regarded as a parameter which is set at the regulatory level. Of the three independent variables IM, IP and OM, the level of industry maturity (IM) and the degree of investment plasticity (IP) are given by the nature of the underlying investment relation, whereas the organizational mode (OM) represents the decision variable at the business level. The efficiency criterion, the amount of investment relation costs (IRC), is the dependent variable. Decision makers at the business level who want to achieve economic efficiency with regard to capital allocation and corporate governance are confronted with the following decision problem:

$$\text{Min } IRC_i = f(RE_i; IM_i; IP_i; OM_i) \qquad (1.5'')$$
$$OMi$$

Below is offered a solution to this decision problem. The comparative efficiency of alternative modes of capital allocation and corporate governance under neoclassical (relational) regulation is analyzed; and the specific problems of a comparative efficiency analysis under hybrid regulatory environments is addressed.

Organizational response to capital market inefficiencies under neoclassical regulation

Neoclassical regulation prevents the creation of financial keiretsu. The banking sector is separated into commercial and investment banks. Commercial banks are precluded from holding equity stakes in non-banks or otherwise exercising non-default control over customer firms.

The separation of banking activities strengthens capital markets by promoting an independent, well-developed and highly innovative investment industry. Strong capital markets are able to aggregate and transmit the individual knowledge of a large number of investors through the price mechanism. The capital market transactions of each individual investor are the result of personal expectations. These expectations in turn result from the investor's individual knowledge set θ_i. As discussed above, each individual knowledge set θ_i may be described as a function of the accurate knowledge set θ_a and an error term ε_i:

$$\theta_i = \theta_a + \varepsilon_i \qquad (1.4)$$

In case of investments into immature industries, it is very likely that the expected value of each error term $E(\varepsilon_i) = 0$ and that the ε_i are independent. Due to a lack of investment history, there is little common knowledge on which investors may base their expectations. Investors have to rely primarily on private knowledge when forming their expectations concerning investment return and risk within immature industries. Each investor's relevant set of private knowledge consists of event and effect information which reflects the investor's area of specialization.

In an economy which is based on the principles of specialization and division of labor, the success of immature industries depends on a wide variety of factors. Without investment experience and industry stability, industry insiders cannot base their investment decisions on complete knowledge about this variety of factors. As long as insiders have to base these decisions on rather incomplete knowledge sets, the associated error terms ε_i will be substantial. If outsiders participate in the process of capital allocation, the sum of all error terms will tend to zero. By participating in capital market transactions, outsiders contribute investment-relevant event and effect information from their respective area of specialization. Since the additional error terms improve information accuracy, capital markets are able to aggregate investment-relevant knowledge which is literally scattered throughout society.

The picture turns as soon as the level of industry maturity increases. While scattered knowledge is of essential importance to the allocation of capital within immature industries, its relevance decreases as an industry moves toward maturity. Mature industries are characterized by high degrees of industry stability. This stability enhances predictability and reduces the importance of scattered knowledge. Consequently, industry insiders enjoy substantial information advantages over outsiders with regard to investments into mature industries. Based on the combination of industry-specific investment experience and insider knowledge, industry insiders are likely to estimate return expectations and investment risk within mature industries more accurately than outsiders. Since scattered knowledge is of little significance compared to common and insider knowledge, including outsiders in the process of allocating capital within mature industries jeopardizes allocative efficiency. Systematic deficiencies of insider knowledge and of industry-specific investment experience will result in biased estimation errors among outsiders. Since these errors have an expected value which is greater than zero, a systematic bias will remain even if all regular errors offset each other as a result of the law of large numbers. Hence, instead of aggregating relevant knowledge, capital markets promote systematic errors by including large numbers of outsiders in the process of allocating capital within mature industries.

As the level of industry maturity increases, unintermediated capital markets gradually lose their accuracy in allocating scarce capital to high-yield uses. Knowledge relevance gradually shifts from scattered to insider knowledge. Fund and bank intermediation allows neoclassical capital markets to retain their accuracy despite the gradual shift in knowledge relevance. Intermediated capital markets are able to accumulate larger shares of insider knowledge in relation to scattered knowledge than are unintermediated capital markets. Consequently, fund and bank intermediation extends the allocative efficiency of capital markets from investments within immature industries to investments within industries characterized by low-to-medium levels of industry maturity.

In the case of investment relations which are characterized by medium-to-high levels of industry maturity, even intermediated capital markets will fail to aggregate the required amounts of insider knowledge in relation to scattered knowledge. Diversification requirements enforced by neoclassical regulation preclude investment companies from acquiring large shares of a single corporation's outstanding stocks or bonds.[54] Commercial banks which are precluded from holding non-default decision rights under neoclassical regulation will prefer to diversify the default risk of their loans. As a result, neither bank nor fund managers will benefit from investing exclusively in firm-specific insider knowledge. Even if bank or fund managers were to focus their information activities on a single firm, diversification requirements would prevent them from realizing the entire information rent.

Since the amount of insider knowledge which is aggregated by intermediated capital markets remains low in relation to the amount of scattered knowledge which is obtained through the participation of outsiders, systematic errors will prevail to a considerable extent. As a result, capital markets will not allocate financial resources efficiently within industries whose level of maturity has reached medium or high levels. Organizational modes which restrict or even exclude outsiders from participating in the process of capital allocation will achieve significantly better results.

Given medium-to-high levels of industry maturity, holding companies and multidivisional organizations have to be considered as efficient organizational responses to allocative inefficiencies of capital markets. While multidivisional organizations eliminate the impact of systematic errors by allocating capital exclusively on the basis of insider (and common) knowledge, holding companies provide an organizational flexibility which allows them to fine-tune the amount of scattered knowledge which is aggregated in addition to the prevailing insider knowledge.

Holding companies which own 100 percent of their subsidiaries' outstanding equity are entitled to allocate 100 percent of their subsidiaries' earnings. Moreover, 100 percent ownership facilitates informal capital transfer among subsidiaries by selling goods or services above or below market prices and by clearing inventories. In this regard, holding companies which own 100 percent of their subsidiaries' outstanding equity do not differ substantially from multidivisional organizations. Both the headquarters of a holding company which owns 100 percent of its subsidiaries' outstanding equity, and the general office of a multidivisional organization, rely exclusively on their insider knowledge in addition to the existing common knowledge when allocating financial resources among their subsidiaries and divisions. Outsiders are effectively excluded from the process of capital allocation among subsidiaries or divisions. As a result, systematic errors will not occur. Consequently, multidivisional organizations and holding companies which own 100 percent of their subsidiaries' outstanding equity are well suited to allocate capital within highly mature industries. Since scattered knowledge has little or no relevance with regard to allocating scarce capital within mature industries, any participation of outsiders in the process of capital allocation would impair allocative efficiency. The participation of outsiders would only produce systematic errors which could be prevented by relying exclusively on insider (and common) knowledge.

Although multidivisional organizations and holding companies which own 100 percent of their subsidiaries' outstanding equity share many common characteristics with regard to capital allocation, multidivisional organizations possess the advantage of unrestricted real-time capital (re)allocation among their divisions. The legal structure of holding companies restricts capital (re)allocation among subsidiaries. Due to informal ways of capital (re)allocation, however, this advantage of multidivisional organizations over holding companies is limited. Nevertheless, it may give multidivisional organizations an edge with regard to allocating capital within highly mature industries.

If the level of industry maturity does not reach very high levels, this advantage will be offset by the fine-tuning abilities of holding companies. By lowering or expanding their equity stocks, holding companies are able to adjust the amounts of scattered and insider knowledge which are accumulated during the process of capital allocation to the specific requirements of each underlying level of industry maturity. For example, holding 90 percent of a subsidiary's outstanding equity could be appropriate if the subsidiary operates in an almost-mature industry, whereas 60 percent ownership would ensure that a substantial amount of scattered knowledge is accumulated during the process of capital allocation in order to meet the knowledge requirements of industries which are characterized by medium levels of maturity.

Less than 100 percent ownership of subsidiaries enables holding companies to benefit from the price signals which are produced by the market mechanism without sacrificing the information advantages associated with ownership concentration. Unlike fund and bank managers, executives of holding companies are not discouraged by diversification requirements to concentrate their information activities on the generation and acquisition of firm-specific knowledge about a very limited number of corporations. Highly concentrated ownership rights guarantee holding companies a fair share of the information rents which are associated with firm-specific knowledge.

So far, organizational choice at the business level under neoclassical regulation has been analyzed solely from the perspective of capital allocation. In order to develop a more comprehensive understanding of the choice effects, the economic analysis must be extended to the area of corporate governance.

Investment relations may be distinguished according to their degree of investment plasticity. The extreme case of completely implastic investments does not cause any governance problems. Opportunism by firm executives is either impossible because the firm's assets can only be used in the desired way,[55] or because it will easily be detected due to costless governance. Given these circumstances, unintermediated market governance will suffice. There is no need to establish more powerful governance structures. Even investments into publicly held corporations with widely dispersed ownership rights will be governed efficiently within unintermediated neoclassical capital markets. Since signaling, screening and monitoring, if necessary, is costless, ownership fragmentation does not result in a governance vacuum. Even small shareholders will benefit from exercising their control rights. Small bondholders are protected against potential opportunism as well. Bond covenants are either unnecessary due to the limited usefulness of the firm's assets, or easily enforceable due to costless monitoring.

Under neoclassical regulation, unintermediated capital markets will achieve governance efficiency not only in the extreme case of completely implastic investments, but also in those cases which are characterized by low degrees of investment plasticity. Extensive, well-specified and well-enforced disclosure and auditing rules assure that the governance advantages which are associated with low levels of investment plasticity do not fall victim to an artificial inflation of screening and monitoring costs. As long as both cost categories remain low, small investors are not economically precluded from exercising their control rights.

If the degree of investment plasticity rises from low to medium levels, unintermediated capital markets will fail to achieve efficient levels of corporate governance. Screening and monitoring costs will increase to a level at which small investors no longer benefit from investing into corporate governance. Publicly held corporations are likely to fall into a governance vacuum—a situation which may easily be exploited by opportunistic executives. In this case, bank and fund intermediation will effectively restore efficient governance structures. Both banks and investment companies (or trusts) possess stronger incentives to conduct screening and monitoring activities than a single small investor. By accumulating the investments of a large number of small investors, banks and investment companies (or trusts) are able to internalize substantial parts of the screening and monitoring benefits which are regularly excluded as externalities from private cost-benefit calculations of small investors in unintermediated capital markets. Competitive forces, reputational effects, bank regulation and the disciplinary consequences of share redemptions and deposit withdrawals assure that the resulting governance benefits will not be completely absorbed by opportunistic bank and fund managers, but will accrue to a fair extent to small investors.

In the case of investment relations whose degree of investment plasticity exceeds medium levels, neither unintermediated nor intermediated capital markets will be able to provide efficient governance structures. In the absence of strong inside governance, medium-to-high levels of investment plasticity open the door to a wide spectrum of discretionary behavior by corporate executives. Individual investors usually do not possess the necessary amounts of capital to acquire ownership majorities which would enable them both economically and legally to provide effective inside governance. Even if individual investors had the necessary amounts of capital, high nondiversification costs in combination with additional burdens imposed by neoclassical regulations such as disclosure requirements,[56] trading restrictions[57] and extended liability[58] would discourage them from acquiring ownership majorities. Commercial banks are not entitled to exercise non-default control over non-banks. Neoclassical diversification requirements[59] prevent investment banks, investment companies and investment trusts, insurance companies and pension funds from accumulating majority stakes in single corporations. Thus persistent corporate governance is neither feasible nor economically rewarding.

Given these circumstances, the potential governance vacuum can only be filled by holding companies or multidivisional organizations. Unless anti-trust regulations apply, holding companies are not restricted from acquiring up to 100 percent of a corporation's outstanding equity; multidivisional organizations may purchase entire firms and integrate them into their divisional structure.

The governance structures within holding companies and multidivisional organizations are more powerful than those provided by commercial banks, investment companies, investment trusts, pension funds or insurance companies. While bank, fund and insurance managers have to keep track of a large number of highly diversified investments, executives of holding companies and multidivisional organizations may concentrate their governance activities on a comparatively small number of subsidiaries or divisions. Corporate governance within holding companies and multidivisional organizations is further facilitated by the fact that both regard their investments into subsidiaries or divisions as long-term investments compared to the rather short-term investments of banks, funds and insurance companies. This long-term orientation not only generates information rents with regard to corporate governance activities, it also lays the foundation for an internal promotion system which rewards the acquisition of corporate-specific human capital and creates long-term loyalty. Internal promotion systems enhance governance efficiency in two ways. They reduce the incentives to behave opportunistically and minimize the information asymmetries between top executives and subsidiary or division managers. Top executives who have served as subsidiary or division managers during their careers possess considerable amounts of experience and insider knowledge which allows them to interpret firm-specific accounting data much more accurately than bank or fund managers.

Powerful enforcement mechanisms are another major advantage of holding companies and multidivisional organizations compared to other organizational modes of capital allocation and corporate governance. While investment companies, investment trusts, pension funds and insurance companies rely on the support of other investors if they want to exercise direct control over a corporation or demand additional information, holding companies, which usually own a majority of their subsidiaries' outstanding equity, are less dependent upon other investors in this respect. Multidivisional organizations enjoy an even larger amount of autonomy. The central office is able to exercise hierarchical control over each division and is entitled to demand information way in excess of neoclassical disclosure obligations. Since establishing and maintaining these hierarchical control mechanisms is very expensive, the potential governance advantages of multidivisional organizations are limited to investment relations which are characterized by high levels of investment plasticity. Holding companies, on the other hand, provide potentially efficient governance structures for investment relations whose degree of plasticity exceeds medium levels but does not reach high levels. Holding companies provide their executives with the unique ability to fine-tune the combination of market and non-market governance by varying the degree to which they own their subsidiaries.

To what extent the efficiency potential of holding companies and multidivisional organizations can actually be realized depends upon the effectiveness with which opportunism at headquarters level is restricted. In other words, governance efficiency at the subsidiary or divisional level is a necessary but not sufficient condition for overall governance efficiency. If the discretionary freedom of executives at headquarters level is not effectively restricted, large parts of the governance advantages which had been realized at the subsidiary or divisional level will not accrue to investors, but will be absorbed by opportunistic executives at headquarters level.

The effectiveness with which opportunism at headquarters level is restricted depends upon the existence and strength of a market for corporate control. A strong market for corporate control exposes top executives of holding companies and multidivisional organizations to strong disciplinary forces. Inefficiencies are likely to be detected by rival management teams which try to gain corporate control via proxy contests or hostile takeovers. Since incumbent managers will suffer severe losses with respect to the value of their corporate-specific human capital when being ousted by rival management teams, they have strong incentives to avoid proxy contests and hostile takeovers by maximizing shareholder wealth. With the innovation of LBOs, even managers of very large corporations are no longer exempted from the disciplinary forces of an active market for corporate control.

If regulations weaken the market for corporate control by promoting anti-takeover devices, governance inefficiencies will prevail. Top executives of holding companies and multidivisional organizations will enjoy at least some discretionary freedom. At the same time it will be more difficult for holding companies and multidivisional organizations to acquire new subsidiaries or divisions. As a result, both modes of corporate governance will lose some of their comparative advantage over intermediated and un-intermediated capital markets.

In order to conclude the efficiency analysis of organizational choice at the business level under neoclassical regulation, potential trade-offs between misallocation costs and governance costs must be assessed. The results are included in Figure 1.9, which matches the relevant characteristics of investment relations and the available modes of capital allocation and corporate governance in an effi-ciency-discriminating manner.

Under neoclassical regulation, capital markets are the efficient mode of capital allocation and corporate governance as long as the under-lying investment relations are characterized by degrees of industry maturity and investment plasticity which do not exceed medium levels. If both characteristics of an investment relation exceed medium levels, but do not reach high levels, holding companies will minimize investment relation costs. In these cases there are no trade-offs.

However, trade-offs do exist in the north-east and south-west quarter of Figure 1.9, and to a lesser extent in the area close to the south-east corner. The north-eastern (south-western) area represents investment relations which are characterized by medium-to-high (low-to-medium) levels of investment plasticity and low-to-medium (medium-to-high) levels of industry maturity. Under these circum-stances, capital markets will promote allocative (governance) efficiency at the expense of governance (allocative) efficiency. Holding companies, on the other hand, will reduce governance (misallocation) costs only by incurring additional misallocation

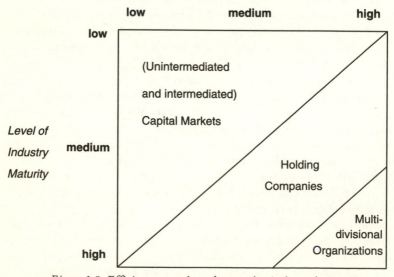

Figure 1.9 Efficiency match under neoclassical regulation

(governance) costs. Figure 1.9 is based on the assumption that both modes of organization can handle trade-offs equally well as long as the underlying investment relation's degree of investment plasticity (industry maturity) exceeds medium levels by the same margin by which its degree of investment maturity (industry plasticity) fails to reach medium levels. If, however, the underlying investment relation's degree of investment plasticity (industry maturity) exceeds medium levels by a larger margin than that by which its degree of industry maturity (investment plasticity) fails to reach medium levels, holding companies will outperform capital markets and vice versa.

Turning to the south-eastern area of Figure 1.9, multidivisional organizations are efficient whenever an investment relation's degrees of investment plasticity and industry maturity reach high levels. Finally, keep in mind that the efficiency border between capital markets and holding companies will move further to the south-eastern (north-western) corner under an inactive (active) market for corporate control.

Organizational response to capital market inefficiencies under relational regulation

Capital allocation and corporate governance under relational regulation are characterized by the weakness of underdeveloped capital markets and the prevailing dominance of privileged universal banks. Relational regulation does not impose legal constraints on bank control over non-banks. Under relational regulation, privileged universal banks may acquire majority equity stakes in non-banks, exercise proxy voting rights and be represented on corporate boards. In this regulatory environment, financial keiretsu are unlikely to evolve. Why should banks commit themselves to a corporate network of minority cross-shareholdings and mutual control if they are entitled to exercise unrestricted unilateral control over other corporations?

As discussed above, universal banks, especially privileged universal banks, enjoy substantial competitive advantages over investment banks. This competitive asymmetry will eventually lead to an erosion of investment banks. Without continuous and strong competition in the investment sector, universal banks will focus their efforts on commercial banking. By repeatedly prolonging loans to industry customers, universal banks are able to realize an ongoing stream of information rents. In order to protect these information rents, universal banks will try to use their influence to prevent industry customers from raising capital via public offerings. As a result, only a very limited number of firms will have direct access to the capital market.

Under relational regulation, small investors are confronted with substantial information disadvantages. Vague and weak accounting, disclosure and auditing rules cement rather than reduce existing information asymmetries. Large investors, on the other hand, benefit from relational regulation. No laws or weak laws against insider trading and market manipulation allow them to profit from information advantages and capital accumulation. Since these profits are realized at the expense of small investors, capital markets will have difficulties attracting a wide spectrum of investors under relational regulation. Many savers will prefer other investment opportunities. Small savers who regard profits from insider trading and market manipulation as a compensation for the governance activities and nondiversification costs of large investors will try to minimize their losses to insiders and market manipulators by focusing on long-term investment strategies. Profits from insider trading and market manipulation which accrue predominantly to large investors may be regarded as additional transaction costs from the perspective of small investors. If small investors want to reduce these costs, they must decrease the turnover ratio of their investment portfolios.

As long as only a very small portion of savers trades frequently, relational capital markets will fail to aggregate large amounts of scattered knowledge. If the number of traders is small and the frequency of trades remains low, individual errors regarding the expected return and risk of investment alternatives are unlikely to offset each other as a result of the law of large numbers. Major errors are likely to prevail. Since these errors will be incorporated into market prices together with relatively small amounts of scattered knowledge, price signals will fail to transmit accurate investment information. Market manipulations may further impair the accuracy of market prices. Consequently, the price mechanism will not allocate scarce equity to its highest yield uses within industries whose degree of industry maturity does not exceed medium levels.

Despite the existence of privileged universal banks, intermediated debt markets cannot prevent the resulting allocative inefficiencies. Even privileged universal banks, which have the potential of exercising non-default decision rights, will refuse to grant loans to corporations which operate in rather immature industries. As long as these corporations are independent, they cannot usually provide sufficient collateral to secure bank loans. Thus banks would be left with unacceptable default risk. If these corporations were subsidiaries of diversified holding companies or divisions of conglomerates, it would be easier for them to meet the demand for collateral. Then, however, capital allocation would rely primarily, if not entirely, on common and insider knowledge. Again, scattered knowledge would not be used effectively.

As a result of the inability to aggregate large amounts of scattered knowledge, relational capital markets would be less effective than neoclassical capital markets with respect to allocating scarce capital to high-yield uses within industries whose degree of maturity does not exceed medium levels. Moreover, under relational regulation, capital markets will lose their comparative advantage over holding companies and multidivisional organizations regarding capital allocation within these industries. Under neoclassical regulation, the comparative advantage of capital markets was based on their unique ability to aggregate and transmit scattered knowledge. As soon as this ability is undermined, the comparative advantage will disappear.

At the same time, relational regulation improves the effectiveness of capital markets in regard to capital allocation within industries whose degree of maturity exceeds medium levels. Ineffective restriction of insider trading enhances the accuracy with which capital market prices reflect available insider knowledge. Since outsiders trade smaller volumes of securities and less frequently than insiders, the amount of insider knowledge which is aggregated and transmitted by the price mechanism under relational regulation is rather large in comparison to the aggregated and conveyed quantity of scattered knowledge.

In addition, relational regulation promotes long-term investment perspectives by encouraging ownership concentration. Contrary to neoclassical regulation, relational regulation does not impose extra burdens (such as extended liability and disclosure obligations) on major shareholders, but rather enables them to maintain and benefit from their information advantage in order to compensate nondiversification costs. Concentrated ownership relieves corporations from constant market pressures to meet short-term profit expectations and pay out regular dividends. A major shareholder who enjoys the benefits of relational regulation will be less reluctant to forego short-term profits in exchange for long-term prospects than will small investors under neoclassical regulation. Even small investors will discount future investment returns at a lower rate under relational regulation than under neoclassical regulation. Under relational regulation, small investors try to avoid losses to insiders or market manipulators by trading less frequently. As a result, the investment perspective of small shareholders is more long-term-oriented under relational than under neoclassical regulation. Under concentrated ownership, long-term investment decisions will be based primarily on common and insider knowledge. As a consequence, relational capital markets effectively allocate scarce capital within mature industries.

With respect to capital allocation within immature industries, long-term investment perspectives would be of benefit as well. Since long-term investment decisions are based primarily on common and insider knowledge under relational regulation, the initial benefits are offset by high misallocation costs. This theoretical result supports the previous conclusion that relational capital markets are less effective in allocating capital within immature industries than are neoclassical capital markets, and in fact do not possess substantial allocative advantages over holding companies or multidivisional organizations.

To refocus on capital allocation within mature industries under relational regulation, the performance of relational capital markets is further improved by the presence of privileged universal banks. The impact of privileged universal banks is threefold. First, proxy voting by privileged universal banks assures that long-term investment decisions are based primarily on common and insider knowledge even if there is no major shareholder. Second, board representation by bank executives creates important knowledge links which provide the corporations involved with otherwise inaccessible investment knowledge. Finally, privileged universal banks may become major shareholders themselves by acquiring large portions of a corporation's outstanding equity.

Under these conditions, there will be no substantial differences between relational capital markets and holding companies or multi-divisional organizations regarding capital allocation within industries whose degree of industry maturity exceeds medium levels. All these organizational modes allocate scarce capital primarily on the basis of common and insider knowledge.

Under relational regulation, the headquarters of a holding

company is not confronted with significant trade-off problems between insider and scattered knowledge when determining what percentage of a subsidiary's outstanding equity should be acquired. Each additional ownership stake shifts allocative responsibility from capital markets to headquarters. While this shift, had it occurred under neoclassical regulation, would base capital allocation to a larger extent on insider knowledge and to a lesser extent on scattered knowledge, it will hardly cause major changes in the composition of knowledge on which the process of capital allocation is founded if it occurs under relational regulation. Besides common knowledge, which has no distinctive consequences for organizational choice, relational capital markets transmit relatively large amounts of insider knowledge compared to the rather limited amount of scattered knowledge which is aggregated by the price mechanism. Consequently, holding companies will lose their fine-tuning ability under relational regulation.

Corporate governance under relational regulation relies primarily on the screening and monitoring activities of major investors and privileged universal banks. Unlike neoclassical regulation, relational regulation does not aim at reducing the information advantages of small investors. Accounting, disclosure and auditing rules are either weak or do not exist. The resulting information asymmetries practically preclude small investors from engaging in corporate governance. Even investment relations which are characterized by low degrees of investment plasticity would cause prohibitively high agency costs if corporate governance had to rely exclusively on the screening and monitoring activities of small investors. However, since relational regulation encourages ownership concentration, relational capital markets will not enter a governance vacuum. Ownership concentration guarantees an efficient level of corporate governance regardless of the prevailing degree of investment plasticity. Large investors possess the incentives to monitor as well as the power to discipline corporate management. Since the potential benefits of corporate governance are positively correlated with the underlying degree of investment plasticity, large investors will respond to high levels of investment plasticity with intense corporate governance.

In case of ownership fragmentation, banks can fill the resulting governance vacuum either by acquiring a considerable amount of equity stake themselves, or through proxy voting and board representation. In addition, banks may discipline corporate management by threatening to deny or withdraw loans.

Consequently, holding companies and multidivisional organizations do not possess significant governance advantages over relational capital markets in case of high levels of investment plasticity. Naturally, bank representatives may act as opportunistically as any other kind of agent. But so do executives of holding companies and multidivisional organizations. If a privileged universal bank holds a substantial amount of a corporation's outstanding equity, bank representatives are in a similar position to holding company executives. An active market for corporate control or ownership concentration at the bank and holding company level effectively constrains the discretionary freedom of bank representatives and holding company executives.

In general, relational regulation supports ownership concentration and corporate takeovers, which are a means of concentrating ownership rights. However, takeovers, especially hostile takeovers, may become unattractive or impossible due to other kinds of regulations. Yet even in the absence of ownership concentration and an active market for corporate control at the bank and holding company level, holding companies do not possess significant governance advantages over bank-intermediated capital markets. Nor do multidivisional organizations. If a holding company or multidivisional organization is publicly held and the market for corporate control is inactive, the only effective way to restrict opportunism at the headquarters' level is bank-intermediation. Proxy voting rights, board representation and credit control enable privileged universal banks to discipline opportunistic executives of publicly held holding companies or multidivisional organizations. But why should holding companies or multidivisional organizations be created if they ultimately rely on the efficiency of the same governance mechanism which they initially intended to replace?

If privileged universal banks fill the governance vacuum which is caused by ownership fragmentation through proxy voting and board representation, their governance activities will not be guided by the same kind of self-interest as under direct or indirect bank ownership. Nevertheless, bank executives do not enjoy unlimited discretionary freedom. Inefficient corporate governance may result in proxy contests which (whether won or lost) are likely to have an extremely negative impact on the reputation of the bank in general and the involved bank representatives in particular.

Special governance problems will arise if bank executives control the shareholder meetings of their own bank through the exercise of proxy voting rights. While smaller privileged universal banks are often privately owned, this kind of self-governance is not atypical for large publicly held banks. Although self-governance may be regarded as a source of unlimited opportunism by bank executives, potential governance inefficiencies are constrained by two forms of non-equity-based governance mechanisms. As Gorton and Schmid (1994: 35) suggest, major executives of large publicly held universal banks are under constant public scrutiny. Society is usually well aware of the economic power which may be exercised by representatives of large publicly held universal banks. As a consequence their actions are monitored through institutions such as the media, unions or even government.

Debt funding provides the foundation for the second non-equity-based governance mechanism. Privileged universal banks are highly leveraged enterprises. Equity represents only a small fraction of total funds. Large amounts of debt put bank executives under current pressure to meet interest and principal obligations. Since customer deposits account for a significant amount of total debt, any loss of reputation will have devastating effects if it results in deposit withdrawals. Nevertheless, some freedom to act opportunistically will remain in most cases. Yet resulting inefficiencies are likely to be offset by low costs of financial distress. Since privileged universal banks are able to intervene and take preventive measures at an early stage of financial distress, bank-dominated governance structures will keep the costs of corporate restructuring at comparatively low levels.

In conclusion, the analysis within this chapter has revealed that relational regulation does not economize on organizational variety. Due to ownership concentration and bank intermediation, there is no constellation of industry maturity and investment plasticity under which holding companies or multidivisional organizations enjoy significant advantages over relational capital markets, and vice versa. It is impossible to discriminate among these modes of capital allocation and corporate governance on the basis of investment relation costs. A number of otherwise secondary reasons contribute to the foundation of holding companies and multidivisional organizations. These reasons include the attempt of major shareholders to benefit from pyramiding effects and the desire of managers to diversify the risk of losing their corporate-specific human capital. In addition, holding companies and multidivisional organizations are often established under relational regulation in an effort to raise capital for smaller firms. Independently, these firms are unable to access the rather underdeveloped relational capital market.

Organizational response to capital market inefficiencies under hybrid regulation

Neoclassical and relational regulations represent the extreme poles of a wide regulatory spectrum. In many cases, hybrid forms of capital market regulation will prevail. These hybrid forms are characterized by a combination of neoclassical and relational elements. Since there is a wide variety of potential combinations, and each particular combination may have specific efficiency impacts, it is impossible to make general predictions about organizational response to capital market inefficiencies under hybrid regulation. A sound evaluation of organizational efficiency has to take account of the prevailing regulatory specifics.

2

EMPIRICAL EVIDENCE FROM GERMANY, JAPAN AND THE UNITED STATES

This chapter reports empirical evidence from Germany, Japan and the United States. For each country in turn there are subsections dealing with

1 comprehensive analysis of the regulatory environment
2 comparative capital market data
3 analysis of the structure and concentration of corporate ownership
4 prediction of the organizational response to capital market inefficiencies on the basis of the theoretical framework developed in Chapter 1
5 the statistical method which is applied to test these predictions
6 the statistical results.

GERMANY

Regulatory environment

Corporate law In order to qualify for stock exchange listing, German companies have to be incorporated as *Aktiengesellschaft* (AG) or *Kommanditgesellschaft auf Aktien* (KGaA). The legal provisions which regulate AGs and KGaAs are contained in the *Aktiengesetz*— the AktG or "Stock Act" of 1965—in the currently valid version of 1985.

A KGaA[1] is a partly limited partnership which combines the characteristics of a partnership with those of a stock corporation. It consists of shareholders whose liability is limited to the nominal value of their shares and at least one partner who is a major executive of the company and has unlimited liability. Compared to AGs,

KGaAs are of minor importance. As of October 1995 there were only eight KGaAs among Germany's 666 listed corporations.

AGs (literally "stock companies") are the German counterpart of US corporations and Japanese *kabushiki-kaisha*. An AG[2] may issue *Stammaktien* (ordinary shares) as well as *Vorzugsaktien* (preference shares). *Stammaktien* entitle their holders to receive a proportionate share of total distributed profits[3] and assets,[4] to demand information,[5] and to vote at the meeting of shareholders.[6] However, the voting rights of any single shareholder, individual or firm may be limited to a maximum number of votes by virtue of the company's constitution.[7] Since 1937 the issue of multiple voting rights has been confined to exceptional cases, and to meet government approval must be considered to serve important overall economic purposes.[8] *Vorzugsaktien* carry preferential rights to cumulative dividends and may be endorsed with or without voting rights.[9]

German AGs have three organs: *Hauptversammlung* (the shareholder meeting), *Vorstand* (the executive board) and *Aufsichtsrat* (the supervisory board). The *Hauptversammlung*[10] is usually held once a year, unless special circumstances (e.g. an intended merger) require otherwise. Most decisions are made by simple majority. These include the discharge of *Vorstand* and *Aufsichtsrat*,[11] the appointment of shareholder representatives to the *Aufsichtsrat*,[12] the appointment of auditors[13] and the appropriation of the annual balance sheet profit.[14] Decisions which require qualified majorities include changes in the company's constitution,[15] capital increases,[16] capital reductions,[17] voluntary liquidation of the company,[18] integration of the company into another AG,[19] mergers[20] and conversion to another legal form.[21]

The *Vorstand*[22] carries full responsibility for managing the company. To fulfill its duties, the *Vorstand* enjoys unlimited representative authority. The chairperson (or speaker) and members of the *Vorstand* are appointed by the *Aufsichtsrat* for a maximum period of five years. Reappointments are possible. The appointment may be revoked for material reasons.

The *Aufsichtsrat*[23] appoints, monitors and if necessary may dismiss the *Vorstand*. *Aufsichtsrat* meetings should be held every three months and must be held at least once a year. As a rule, the *Aufsichtsrat* decides by simple majority. The chairperson and members of the *Aufsichtsrat* need not be shareholders and must not be members of the *Vorstand*. As compensation for their activities the chairperson and members of the *Aufsichtsrat* may receive appropriate emoluments. Originally designed to represent the interests of share-holders, the *Aufsichtsrat* has become an instrument to settle a company's internal conflicts between capital (shareholders) and labor (employees) under German codetermination laws.

The scope of mandatory codetermination is defined by the *Montanmitbestimmungsgesetz* of 1951 (MontanMitbestG), the *Montanmitbestimmungsergänzungsgesetz* of 1956, the *Mitbestimmungsgesetz* of 1976 (MitbestG) and the *Betriebsverfassungsgesetz* of 1952/1972 (BetrVG). According to the BetrVG (or "Company Constitution Act") every company with at least five employees must have a work council elected by the employees and composed exclusively of employees. The decision rights of the work council are restricted to personnel and social issues. The function of the work council is to assure that management searches for socially acceptable solutions to economic challenges. If the work council refuses to approve measures which require statutory approval, the final decision will be transferred to a company conciliation board or a court of law. In addition to the implementation of work councils, the BetrVG regulates the composition of the *Aufsichtsrat* in companies with more than 500 employees.[24] The BetrVG requires that one-third of the *Aufsichtsrat* members are elected by employees. Since the *Aufsichtsrat* decides by simple majority, however, shareholder representatives remain in control.

Quasi-parity codetermination is enforced by the MitbestG ("Codetermination Act"). It applies to companies with more than 2,000 employees.[25] According to the Act, exactly half of the *Aufsichtsrat* members must be employee representatives, including labor union representatives, and there must be at least one company executive to represent executive employees. In order to prevent paralyzation of corporate decision making, the chairperson of the *Aufsichtsrat* is granted a second vote in deadlock situations. The chairperson of the *Aufsichtsrat* and all *Vorstand* members must be elected by a two-thirds majority. However, this rule applies only to the first ballot. Consequently, the chairperson's second vote becomes decisive in a second ballot of *Vorstand* elections. Since the chairperson is elected by shareholder representatives in the case of a second ballot, capital (the shareholders) still remains in control under quasi-parity codetermination.

Furthermore, the MitbestG establishes personnel and social issues at the *Vorstand* level by introducing an *Arbeitsdirektor* ("labor director"). The *Arbeitsdirektor* is elected to and voted out of office like all other *Vorstand* members.

Full-parity codetermination is required by the MontanMitbestG ("Coal, Iron and Steel Industries Codetermination Act") and its amendment. The MontanMitbestG reflects the traditionally strong political influence of Germany's most powerful labor union. The regulations contained in the MontanMitbestG and its amendment apply to all companies in the coal, iron and steel industry which are incorporated as AG or GmbH and have more than 1,000 employees. The *Aufsichtsrat* of these companies must be composed of a neutral member and an equal number of shareholder and employee representatives. Employee representatives include labor union representatives. Executive employees are not represented separately. Every *Aufsichtsrat* member has one vote. Decisions are made by simple majority (with one exception: the labor director cannot be appointed or dismissed against the vote of a majority of employee representatives). In the case of deadlock situations, the vote of the neutral member is decisive. The neutral member must be elected by a majority of the shareholder and employee representatives.

In general, mandatory codetermination has to be regarded as economically inefficient, because it deprives shareholders and employees of the right to allocate non-default decision rights to the highest yield user. In particular, mandatory codetermination increases the cost of equity, because it transfers non-default decision rights from shareholder to employee representatives. Non-default decision rights are an important instrument for reducing equity risk. Collateralization, on the other hand, which is the major device for reducing credit risk, remains unaffected by mandatory codetermination. Consequently, the debt-equity ratio is likely to increase in response to codetermination.

Accounting, disclosure and auditing rules   German disclosure and auditing rules are based on a creditor-oriented and tax-dominated accounting system. Following the tradition of Roman law, German accounting standards are defined by codified legal provisions which are contained in the *Handelsgesetzbuch* (the HGB or "Commercial Code") of 1897 in its currently valid version of 1985 and in the AktG. Creditor protection is enforced by the realization principle,[26] the lower-of-cost-and-market-value principle,[27] the imparity principle[28] and the provision of mandatory reserves for AGs and KGaAs.[29]

According to the realization principle, any anticipation of positive profit contributions is prohibited. All assets, including long-term financial investments, must be valued at historic costs (minus depreciation) or, if lower, at market value. All liabilities must be valued at the amount at which they are repayable. Inflation accounting is illegal under German law. In compliance with the imparity principle, expected but not yet realized negative profit contributions must be anticipated. These principles usually result in substantial hidden reserves. In addition, the AktG requires the formation of mandatory reserves. AGs and KGaAs must retain 5 percent of their annual balance sheet profits until accumulated reserves equal at least 10 percent of the nominal value of the corporation's outstanding equity. Corporate statutes may contain provisions for additional statutory reserves.

Germany's tax code permits companies to depreciate certain assets in excess of the depreciation methods provided for by the Commercial Code. Since tax accounts have to be based on the asset valuation method chosen within commercial accounts, however, German companies cannot claim the tax benefits associated with the valuation options granted by the tax code unless they chose these valuation methods for commercial accounting.[30] As a result, asset valuation within commercial accounting is predominated by tax considerations. Assets will regularly be undervalued and balance sheet profits will not accurately reflect a company's financial and economic performance.

Creditor orientation and predominance of tax considerations in commercial accounting attenuate the rights of equity owners. As residual claimants they cannot appropriate corporate profits, which are retained as mandatory and statutory reserves or concealed as hidden reserves.

German accounting, disclosure and auditing regulations contain special provisions for AGs, KGaAs and GmbHs[31] as well as large companies.[32] The provisions must guarantee that the annual report conveys a realistic picture of the reporting company's economic and financial situation. In particular, annual reports must consist of balance sheet, income statement, annotation and situational report,[33] are subject to compulsory audits[34] and must be publicly disclosed.[35] Layout, structure and content of balance sheet and income statement must comply with strict provisions.[36] Annotations must contain, among other things, information about the applied reporting, valuation, depreciation and foreign currency translation methods or changes therein,[37] the impact of tax considerations on reported earnings,[38] *Vorstand* and *Aufsichtsrat* compensations,[39] credits granted to

Vorstand and *Aufsichtsrat* members,[40] segmented revenue data for major product lines and geographic areas,[41] the amount of own shares held by the company,[42] equity holdings of more than 20 percent (including recent annual financial results of subsidiaries)[43] and average number of employees.[44] The situational report covers important events which have occurred after the accounting period, expected future developments, and research and development activities.[45] Parent companies have to consolidate their accounts and must publish consolidated annual reports.[46] AGs and KGaAs which are listed on a German stock exchange must publish semi-annual reports in addition to the annual reports.[47] However, semi-annual reports must only contain semi-annual revenues and profits (or losses).[48] Further information regarding the company's general economic and financial situation must be included.[49] Semi-annual reports are not subject to compulsory audits. All companies which have issued stocks or bonds on a German exchange are required to immediately report material (stock price relevant) information.[50]

Compared to US accounting standards, German regulations contribute substantially less to the reduction of information asymmetries between company insiders and outsiders. In particular, German regulations lag behind US standards with respect to the frequency and presentation of accounting information. While US standards require quarterly reports on investment relevant accounting data, German investors have to rely primarily on annual information. German provisions for half yearly reports are weak compared to US standards for quarterly reports.

While the amount of information contained in German annual reports is comparable to US standards, its form of presentation is not. Under German regulations, corporations are not obliged to report earnings per share and changes in shareholder equity. Moreover, German corporations do not have to report selective financial data from previous periods to highlight significant trends. Due to the wide variety of accounting options and the predominance of tax considerations, retrieving investment-relevant information from annual accounts of German companies requires advanced accounting skills and a considerable amount of effort.

Laws against insider trading   Small investors are further disadvantaged by the weak regulations which apply to insider trading and market manipulation. Contrary to US regulations, German corporate insiders do not have to disclose their security trades.

Only since 1995 have major shareholders been obliged to report holdings in voting stock of a listed corporation if these holdings exceed or fall below 5, 10, 25, 50, or 75 percent of total voting rights.[51]

In July 1994, the German legislature passed a law against insider trading in an effort to comply with the European Council Directive 89/592 of 1989 requiring all members of the European Community to prohibit insider trading. According to the new law, insiders who trade securities on the basis of unpublished material event information, tip unpublished material event information, or recommend trades on the basis of unpublished material event information may be sanctioned by fines or imprisonment of up to five years.[52]

Prior to this law, German insider trading restriction relied exclusively on voluntary, privately enforced commitments. As reported by Kohler (1991: 268), about 85 percent of Germany's listed corporations obliged their management to refrain from insider trading and declared all insider gains as fully recoverable by the corporation.

Given this history, the *Bundesaufsichtsamt für den Wertpapierhandel* (Germany's SEC) has little experience in detecting insider trades. Unlike the SEC, the *Bundesaufsichtsamt für den Wertpapierhandel* has to enforce the new insider regulations without supportive insider disclosure regulations. Despite recent legal improvements, Germany's insider trading law enforcement must be regarded as weak compared to US standards.

Laws against market manipulation Prevention of market manipulation suffers from even larger deficiencies. Besides a 1995 rule which prohibits investment service companies to recommend security trades in an effort to influence market prices in favor of their own trades,[53] German laws contain no explicit restrictions on market manipulation. Prohibition of market manipulation relies primarily on general rules of conduct which forbid corporate officials to publish incomplete, false or misleading information and oblige investment advisors to act in their clients' best interest.

(Anti-) takeover regulation The vast majority of corporate takeovers in Germany are friendly. In fact Germany's first hostile takeover did not occur until 1989.[54] There are a variety of reasons which explain the rarity of hostile takeovers (see for example Drukarczyk 1993: 646). First, German corporate law and codetermination requirements prevent successful bidders from taking immediate and complete control of the target corporation. According to German corporate law, members of the *Vorstand* are elected for up to five years and cannot be dismissed without cause.[55] Codetermination limits the non-default decision rights of corporate owners, especially with regard to corporate restructuring. Second, many German corporations are already governed by majority ownership and as a consequence are not a typical target for corporate raiders. Third, most publicly held corporations are controlled by a universal bank through the exercise of proxy voting rights and *Aufsichtsrat* representation. Since the universal bank usually takes the role of the corporation's main creditor (*Hausbank*) it will resist hostile takeovers in order to secure its information rent. Finally, some of Germany's large publicly held corporations have passed corporate statutes which limit the voting rights of single investors.[56] Under these circumstances, German legislators have not come under political pressure to enact additional anti-takeover laws.

Contrary to hostile takeovers, friendly takeovers are encouraged by German regulations. Unless corporate statutes mandate otherwise, corporate takeovers require the approval of a three-quarters majority of the votes cast at the shareholder meeting.[57] Shareholders of the acquired corporation are usually compensated by shares of the acquiring corporation. The exchange rate is determined by the *Vorstand* of both corporations on the basis of the respective corporate values and must be approved by special auditors.[58] This procedure relieves acquiring corporations from the pressure of paying large takeover premiums.

Diversification requirements   German diversification requirements for financial intermediaries are less restrictive than US regulations. German banks are not subject to any diversification requirements. Investment companies are not allowed to invest more than 5 percent (under certain circumstances less than 10 percent) of their assets into the securities of a single issuer.[59] Insurance companies may not, as a rule, acquire more than 10 percent of a corporation's outstanding stock.[60] However, this regulation contains several loopholes. For example, these investment restrictions apply only to an insurance company's devoted capital. Moreover, reinsurance companies and insurance holding companies are not subjected to the 10 percent rule.[61]

Germany's pension system consists of private pension insurance, company pension plans and public pension insurance. Funds accumulated through private pension insurance are subject to the general diversification requirements for insurance companies. The funds accumulated by company pension plans are usually invested within the company itself. Public pension insurance, which is mandatory for all low- and middle-income employees, does not accumulate any capital at all. The entire proceeds are used to pay current beneficiaries. Since public pension insurance is by far the most dominant form of pension insurance, Germany's pension system contributes little to the accumulation and investment of capital.

Restrictions on universal banking   Contrary to Japanese and US regulations, German regulations do not restrict universal banking. German banks are entitled to engage in commercial and investment banking activities.[62] In addition, German banks are not restricted from holding equity stakes in non-banks, being represented on corporate boards (*Aufsichtsrat*) and executing proxy voting rights. According to the so-called *Vollmachtsstimmrecht*, a bank is entitled to vote on behalf of a customer for all shares this customer deposited with the bank if the customer entrusts the bank to do so.[63] The authorization must be made in written form (usually by postcard), may be rescinded at any time and, if not rescinded, remains valid for a maximum period of fifteen months, after which it may be renewed.[64] Prior to a corporation's shareholder meeting, the bank has to inform entrusting customers about the position it takes and the way it intends to vote on each of the agenda's topics.[65] It further has to solicit instructions from entrusting customers with respect to each of the agenda's topics and must disclose whether any of the bank's *Vorstand* members have been elected to the corporation's *Aufsichtsrat* or any of the corporation's *Vorstand* members have been elected to the bank's *Aufsichtsrat*.[66] If the entrusting customer decides not to give any directions the bank must vote as intended unless it is in the entrusting customer's best interest to vote otherwise.[67] At its own shareholder meeting, the bank may exercise its *Vollmachtsstimmrecht* only if the entrusting customer gives directions for each topic.[68]

Federal bank regulation in Germany focuses primarily on the adequacy of capital. The ratio of loans and investments to liable capital many not exceed eighteen to one.[69] Deposit insurance is provided by the *Vereinigung Deutscher Geschäftsbanken* (Association of German Commercial Banks), a privately managed but publicly regulated association.[70]

Conclusion Despite the recent introduction of neoclassical elements (e.g. prohibition of insider trading) Germany's capital market regulation is still deeply rooted in its relational tradition. Capital allocation and investment governance is dominated by large privileged universal banks. In an effort to secure the information rents resulting from commercial loans, Germany's privileged universal banks have undermined the development of Germany's financial markets. Specialized investment banks have been unable to establish themselves in Germany's regulatory environment. Financial innovations, the primary source of profits in the investment banking industry, have effectively dried up. Without competition from specialized investment banks, Germany's privileged universal banks have focused on their lending activities and realized information rents by engaging in long-term relationships with their customers.

Germany's capital market in comparison

Table 2.1 documents the underdevelopment of Germany's financial markets. There were only 666 listed AGs and KGaAs at the end of 1994. Total market capitalization amounted to $499.7 billion, or 11.5 percent of Germany's GDP, compared to $3,600.6 billion (76.5 percent) in Japan and $5,018.7 billion (74.5 percent) in the United States. Adjusted for intercorporate shareholdings, market capitalization reduces to $179.9 billion or 4.1 percent for Germany, $1,281.8 billion (27.1 percent) for Japan and $4,737.7 billion (70.3 percent) for the United States.[71] The actual difference in size between German and Japanese or US equity markets is even larger considering that the data for Germany are based on all domestic corporations which are listed on at least one of Germany's eight stock exchanges,[72] whereas the data for Japan (the US) are limited to domestic corporations listed on the TSE (NYSE and NASDAQ).

Stock market liquidity is low compared to international standards. In 1994, Germany's fifty largest listed AGs and KGaAs accounted for 89.9 percent of total turnover. Of total turnover, 50 percent resulted from trades in Deutsche Bank, Daimler Benz, Siemens, Allianz, Volkswagen and VEBA. Trading volume for these six corporations ranged from $52.6 billion (VEBA) to $145.0 billion (Deutsche Bank) in 1994. Trading volumes of all other German corporations do not reach US and Japanese standards. Equity shares of most German corporations are traded in rather thin markets.

Table 2.1 A comparison of German, Japanese and US capital markets

	Germany	Japan	US
Stock market			
Number of listed domestic corporations[a]	666	1689	6923
Market capitalization of listed domestic corporations (in billion dollars)[a]	499.7	3600.6	5018.7
Market capitalization adjusted for intercorporate-shareholdings[a]	179.9	1281.8	4737.7
Market capitalization as a percentage of GDP[a]	11.5	76.5	74.5
Adjusted market capitalization as a percentage of GDP[a]	4.1	27.1	70.3
Bond market			
Nominal value of outstanding bonds (in billion dollars)	1940.9	4394.9	5885.4
Nominal value of outstanding bonds as a percentage of GDP	44.7	93.4	87.4
Nominal value of outstanding bonds issued by (percentage of total in parentheses):			
Government and government agencies	793.6 (40.9%)	3090.0 (70.3%)	3465.6 (58.9%)
Private financial enterprises	925.0 (47.7%)[b]	789.5 (18.0%)	947.2 (16.1%)
Private nonfinancial enterprises	2.0 (0.1%)	432.8 (9.8%)	251.7 (21.3%)
Foreign institutions	220.3 (11.4%)	82.6 (1.9%)	220.9 (3.8%)
Debt-equity ratio of domestic corporations	2.83[c]	3.98[d]	0.87[d]

All data as of year-end 1994 unless noted otherwise
a For Germany, all exchanges; for Japan, TSE; for US, NYSE and NASDAQ
b includes local and state savings banks
c 1993 data based on all listed domestic nonfinancial corporations
d 1991 data based on all domestic nonfinancial corporations

Sources: Reports of the respective stock exchanges, corporate annual reports, *Monthly Report of the Deutsche Bundesbank*, flow of funds accounts—outstandings unadjusted, Koushasai Geppou, OECD main economic indicators, *OECD Financial Statistics Monthly*, own calculations

The nominal value of outstanding bonds equaled $1,940.9 billion or 44.7 percent of Germany's GDP compared to $4,394.9 billion (93.4 percent) in Japan and $5,885.4 billion (87.4 percent) in the United States. Unlike Japanese and US bond markets, Germany's bond market is dominated by private financial enterprises (including local and state savings banks). They account for 47.7 percent of all outstanding bonds. This dominance reflects Germany's high level of bank intermediation. In Japan and in the United States, private financial institutions account for only 18.0 percent and 16.1 percent respectively.

Germany's private nonfinancial enterprises do not directly access primary debt markets. In Germany, private nonfinancial enterprises account for only 0.1 percent of all outstanding bonds compared to 9.8 percent in Japan and 21.3 percent in the United States. Nevertheless, Germany's listed nonfinancial enterprises are well leveraged. The average debt-equity ratio of Germany's listed nonfinancial enterprises is 2.83. These data suggest that corporate finance relies heavily upon bank intermediation and that German companies are not subjected to credit rationing.

Structure and concentration of corporate ownership

Germany's relational capital market regulation keeps small investors from directly investing in the stock market and encourages ownership intermediation as well as ownership concentration. Table 2.2 compares the ownership structure of listed corporations in Germany, Japan and the US.

In Germany, 17 percent of the outstanding shares of all listed corporations are directly owned by domestic households, compared to 23.5 percent in Japan and 49.8 percent in the US. To be sure, in the absence of complete cross-shareholdings, all shares, except those held by foreign investors, are directly or indirectly owned by domestic households. However, form and size of ownership intermediation may differ from country to country. In Germany ownership intermediation amounts to 64 percent of total shareholdings, compared to 68.6 percent in Japan and 43.9 percent in the US. Domestic enterprises account for 42 percent of Germany's ownership intermediation, whereas pension funds (banks and enterprises) are the major form of ownership intermediation in the US (Japan).

Corporate ownership is highly concentrated in Germany. As shown in Table 2.3, almost three out of four listed corporations have

Table 2.2 Ownership structure of listed corporations in
Germany, Japan and the US

	Germany (1990) %	Japan (1994) %	US (1992) %
Households	17	23.5	49.8
Banks	10	22.2	0.3
Insurance companies	12	17.0	5.0
Pension funds	n.a.	1.6	29.2[a]
Mutual funds	n.a.	-	9.0
Investment trusts	-	2.6	-
Securities companies	-	1.4	0.3[b]
Nonfinancial enterprises	42	23.8	n.a.
Government	5	0.5	0.0
Foreign	14	7.4	6.3

a including state and local government retirement funds
b brokers and dealers

Source: Deutsche Bundesbank, Zenkoku Shoken Torihikijo Kyogikai, US flow of funds

a major shareholder who controls at least 50 percent of the voting rights. In comparison, only a very small fraction of Japanese and US listed corporations have a majority shareholder.

The high level of ownership concentration does not automatically lead to an increase in the cost of capital. Of course, being a large shareholder means to forgo the advantages of holding a well-diversified portfolio. Hence, normal risk aversion implies that investors will purchase large blocks of shares "only at lower risk-compensating prices" (Demsetz and Lehn 1985: 1158). However, the monitoring benefits realized by large shareholders may induce small shareholders to buy shares at a premium which might offset the risk compensation demanded by large shareholders.

Due to the governance activities which are exercised by Germany's

Table 2.3 Ownership concentration under relational
(Germany), hybrid (Japan) and neoclassical (US)
capital market regulation (percentages of total)

Percentage of voting rights (x) controlled by the largest shareholder[a]	Germany[b](1994) %	Japan[c] (1995) %	US[d] (1994) %
0 < x < 10	3.2	61.1	66.0
10 ≤ x < 25	6.9	21.3	17.4
25 ≤ x < 50	16.7	12.9	13.0
50 ≤ x < 75	31.9	4.7	2.1
75 ≤ x ≤ 100	41.3	-	1.5

a including officers and directors as a group; excluding ESOP
b data based on Germany's 550 largest listed AGs and KGaAs
c data based on all 1,321 Japanese *kabushiki-kaisha* listed in the first sections of the Tokyo, Osaka and Nagoya stock exchanges
d data based on all US corporations included in the S&P 500, S&P MidCap 400 and S&P SmallCap 600

Source: own calculations

privileged universal banks on behalf of small shareholders who deposit their shares with the bank, even large publicly held AGs are usually closely monitored. The most detailed empirical information about *Aufsichtsrat* representation and proxy voting by German banks is contained in a report by Germany's Anti-trust Commission (Monopolkommission 1978). This report is based on data from 1974 of Germany's 100 largest corporations (in terms of turnover). According to the report, banks represented more than 5 percent of total voting rights in fifty-five of the 100 corporations. On average,[73] banks controlled 57 percent of the voting rights which were present at the shareholder meeting—about 7 percent through equity holdings and 50 percent based on proxy voting rights (Monopolkommission 1978: 295). The other forty-five corporations all had a dominant shareholder.[74]

Banks were represented on the supervisory board (*Aufsichtsrat*) of seventy-five of the 100 corporations. A bank representative was elected chairperson of the Supervisory Board (*Aufsichtsratsvorsitzender*) in thirty-one corporations, and deputy chairperson in thirty-five corporations. In total, bank representatives held 179 or 15 percent of all 1,203 supervisory board seats (Monopolkommission 1978: 301–5). However, since banks were represented on the supervisory board of only seventy-five of the 100 largest corporations, these figures underestimate the extent of supervisory board representation by German banks. With respect to the seventy-five corporations with bank representation on the supervisory board, banks averaged 2.4 seats and bank representatives accounted for 20 percent of the supervisory board members.

The report further revealed that Germany's three largest private banks, Deutsche Bank, Dresdner Bank and Commerzbank, accounted for 68 percent of the supervisory board chairpersons who were bank representatives, 54 percent of the deputy chairpersons who were bank representatives, and 57 percent of all bank representatives on the supervisory boards of Germany's 100 largest corporations. Among the three big banks, Deutsche Bank, Germany's largest bank, holds a dominant position by accounting for 58 percent of the supervisory board chairpersons who were bank representatives, 31 percent of the deputy chairpersons who were bank representatives, and 31 percent of all bank representatives on the supervisory boards of Germany's 100 largest corporations.

A more recent study by Böhm (1992) confirms the importance of proxy voting and board representation by Germany's privileged universal banks. Based on 1986 data on seven of Germany's largest publicly held corporations, Böhm (1992: 244, Table 26) found that banks controlled on average[75] 80 percent of the voting rights represented at the shareholder meeting. Böhm further surveyed 1986 data on Germany's 100 largest companies (in terms of turnover) in order to find empirical evidence documenting the influence of German banks on large German enterprises. In 1986, sixty-nine out of the 100 largest companies were corporations (AGs or KGaAs). Banks were represented on the supervisory board of sixty-two of the sixty-nine corporations. With respect to these sixty-two corporations, bank representatives held 140 or 13 percent of the 1,090 supervisory board seats.[76] This percentage is significantly lower than the respective percentage (20 percent) in the earlier study by Germany's Anti-trust Commission. However, this difference does not reveal a substantial decline in the role of German banks as delegated monitors on behalf of shareholders, but results primarily from the introduction of the

MitbestG (Codetermination Act) in 1976. In many of Germany's large corporations, the introduction of the MitbestG reduced the number of shareholder representatives on the supervisory board (*Aufsichtsrat*) from two-thirds to one-half of total seats.

In accordance with the earlier study, Germany's three largest private banks accounted for a majority of the chairpersons (65 percent), deputy chairpersons (100 percent) and members (63 percent) of the supervisory board who were bank representatives. Again, Deutsche Bank was by far the most dominant bank, accounting for 50 percent of the chairpersons, all the deputy chairpersons and 35 percent of the ordinary supervisory board members who were bank representatives.

While the percentage of all outstanding shares held directly by German households decreased from 27 percent in 1960 to 17 percent in 1990, share ownership by German banks consistently increased, from 6 percent in 1960 to 10 percent in 1990.[77] Besides Germany's privileged universal banks, insurance companies have emerged as an important financial intermediary. The percentage of all outstanding shares which is held by insurance companies quadrupled in only thirty years, from 3 percent in 1960 to 12 percent in 1990.[78]

Organizational response

As discussed in Chapter 1, ownership concentration and the dominance of privileged universal banks (and insurance companies) enhance corporate governance within relational capital markets. Even in case of high degrees of investment plasticity, multidivisional organizations and holding companies do not enjoy significant governance advantages over relational capital markets. On the other hand, ownership concentration sacrifices the efficiency of capital markets with regard to allocating scarce capital within immature industries. Without the participation of a large number of investors, capital markets will be unable to aggregate and transmit sufficient amounts of scattered knowledge. In a competitive international environment, successful new or immature industries are unlikely to emerge under relational capital market regulation. Empirical evidence from Germany supports this hypothesis. Despite its overall economic importance, Germany does not have competitive biotechnology, information technology, entertainment or business services industries.

While ownership concentration and the resulting small number of capital market participants impair the efficiency of relational capital markets with regard to allocating scarce capital within immature industries, they improve capital allocation within industries whose level of maturity exceeds medium levels. Since a small number of capital market participants further eliminates most of the allocative differences between holding companies and multidivisional organizations, relational regulation does not economize on organizational diversity. Under relational regulation, capital markets, holding companies and multidivisional organizations do not enjoy significant allocation and governance advantages over each other, regardless of the underlying levels of industry maturity and investment plasticity. The following section presents an empirical test of this hypothesis.

Statistical test

With respect to Germany's relational regulation, theory suggests that the prevailing organizational modes of capital allocation and corporate governance do not depend upon the underlying allocation problems and governance hazards. This conjecture will have to be refuted if a significant correlation between the prevailing organizational modes and the underlying coordination problems can be established.

As discussed in Chapter 1, the basic unit of analysis is the investment relation between a firm, defined as a potentially independent production and marketing unit, and investors. In Germany, investment relations may be coordinated by the relational capital market, within a holding company or within a multidivisional organization.

In an effort to establish a statistical relationship between the prevailing organizational mode of capital allocation and corporate governance on the one hand, and the allocation problems and governance hazards associated with the underlying investment relation on the other, the prevailing organizational mode of capital allocation and corporate governance is modeled as a categorical dependent variable. Since this (potentially) dependent variable can take on one of three ordered values and the independent variable (the sum of the underlying allocation problems and governance hazards) is not directly observable, the ordered probit model is used for the statistical analysis.[79] This model, which is estimated using the LIMDEP ordered probit routine, is specified as follows:

$$Z_i = \beta_0 + \beta_1 X_{i1} + \beta_2 X_{i2} + \varepsilon_i \qquad (2.1)$$

where Z_i is an unobservable measure of the allocation problems and governance hazards of investment relation i, β_0 represents a constant term, X_{i1} is the level of industry maturity of investment relation i, X_{i2} is the level of investment plasticity of investment relation i, β_1 and β_2 are the weights attached to each characteristic and ε_i is a random error term with $\varepsilon_i \sim N\,[0,1]$.[80] The observable counterpart to Z_i is the organizational mode $MODE_i$ which is used to coordinate the respective investment relation i.

The level of industry maturity is measured on a scale from one to five, with one indicating an immature industry and five indicating a mature industry. The relation of the sum of research and development expenditures and service-related sales to total revenues is used as a proxy for the level of investment plasticity.

Since there are no empirical studies which attempt to measure the level of investment plasticity, the statistical test cannot build on existing experience. The relation of the sum of research and development expenditures and service-related sales to total revenues seems to be a solid proxy because it captures the relative size of two highly plastic fields of investment. Research and development investments offer managers a wide spectrum of choice alternatives and result in a high level of information asymmetry between principals and agents. Business activities within the service sector rely to a large extent, if not exclusively, on human capital. Since high levels of investment plasticity result primarily from investments into human capital, the relation of service-related sales to total revenues approximates the relative size of investments into human capital.

Another advantage of this proxy is the availability of standardized data. In most cases, standardized data on research and development expenditures, service-related sales and total sales are available. As a result, measurement problems are kept at a minimum.

The organizational mode used to coordinate an investment relation i ($MODE_i$) is modeled as a function of the sum of allocation problems and governance hazards (Z_i) by assuming that the unobservable variable Z_i can be broken up into three discrete intervals each of which corresponds with a different category of $MODE_i$:

If $Z_i < \mu_0$ then $MODE_i = 0$ (relational capital market organization)

If $\mu_0 \leq Z_i < \mu_1$ then $MODE_i = 1$ (holding company organization)

If $\mu_1 \leqslant Z_i$ then $\text{MODE}_i = 2$ (multidivisional organization) (2.2)

The objective of the statistical analysis is twofold: (a) to estimate β_0, β_1 and β_2, the parameters by which the characteristics of an investment relation (X_{i1}, X_{i2}) get translated into allocation problems and governance hazards (Z_i), and (b) to translate each Z_i into one of the three ordered categories of MODE_i. The latter task is equivalent with estimating the threshold variables μ_0 and μ_1.

The probabilities of the independent variable Z_i to fall into the three categories of the dependent variable MODE_i may be written as:

$$P\,(\text{MODE}_i = 0 \mid X_{i1}, X_{i2}) = P[\varepsilon_i < (\mu_0 - \beta_0 - \beta_1 X_{i1} - \beta_2 X_{i2}) \mid X_{i1}, X_{i2}]$$

$$= F(\mu_0 - \beta_0 - \beta_1 X_{i1} - \beta_2 X_{i2})$$

$$P\,(\text{MODE}_i = 1 \mid X_{i1}, X_{i2}) = P[(\mu_0 - \beta_0 - \beta_1 X_{i1} - \beta_2 X_{i2})$$

$$\leqslant \varepsilon_i < (\mu_1 - \beta_0 - \beta_1 X_{i1} - \beta_2 X_{i2}) \mid X_{i1}, X_{i2}]$$

$$= F(\mu_1 - \beta_0 - \beta_1 X_{i1} - \beta_2 X_{i2}) - F(\mu_0 - \beta_0 - \beta_1 X_{i1} - \beta_2 X_{i2})$$

$$P\,(\text{MODE}_i = 2 \mid X_{i1}, X_{i2}) = P[\varepsilon_i \geqslant (\mu_1 - \beta_0 - \beta_1 X_{i1} - \beta_2 X_{i2}) \mid X_{i1}, X_{i2}]$$

$$= 1 - F(\mu_1 - \beta_0 - \beta_1 X_{i1} - \beta_2 X_{i2}) \qquad (2.3)$$

where $F(\bullet)$ denotes the cumulative normal distribution function corresponding to the distribution of the random variable ε_i. In case of the ordered probit model, this is a standard normal distribution.

An additional normalization is necessary to estimate the unknown threshold variables μ_0 and μ_1. Following common practice, μ_0 is set to $\mu_0 = 0$. This leads to:

$$\varphi\text{MODE}_i = 0 \mid X_{i1}, X_{i2}) = \varphi(-\beta_0 - \beta_1 X_{i1} - \beta_2 X_{i2})$$

$$\varphi\,(\text{MODE}_i = 1 \mid X_{i1}, X_{i2}) = \varphi(\mu_1 - \beta_0 - \beta_1 X_{i1} - \beta_2 X_{i2}) - \varphi(-\beta_0 - \beta_1 X_{i1} - \beta_2 X_{i2})$$

$$\varphi(\text{MODE}_i = 2 \mid X_{i1}, X_{i2}) = 1 - \varphi(\mu_1 - \beta_0 - \beta_1 X_{i1} - \beta_2 X_{i2}) \qquad (2.4)$$

where $\varphi(\bullet)$ denotes the cumulative distribution for a standardized normal variable.

Statistical results

The empirical results for Germany are based on a random sample of n = 31 AGs and KGaAs out of all listed nonfinancial AGs and KGaAs. The necessary data have been obtained through questionnaires and the analysis of annual reports and other corporate publications. Unfortunately, some corporations refused to provide the necessary data. Each of these was replaced by another randomly selected corporation. Appendix A of this book lists the names of all corporations included in the sample.

Strictly following the theoretical framework developed in Chapter 1, the random sample of investment relations should have been selected out of all divisions, subsidiaries and independent corporations. Corporations with a multidivisional structure and holding companies should not have been included in the sample. Corporations which are subsidiaries of a holding company should have been categorized as $MODE_i = 1$, divisions as $MODE_i = 2$. However, it is impossible to obtain individual data for single divisions. So the sample consists of corporations, not single divisions. In addition, the sample may include subsidiaries of holding companies as well as holding companies. All holding companies and all subsidiaries of holding companies are classified as "holding company organization" ($MODE_i = 1$), all multidivisional organizations as "multidivisional organization" ($MODE_i = 2$) and all other corporations as "capital market organization" ($MODE_i = 0$).

This procedure does not impair the validity of the empirical test. If firms which are characterized by high levels of investment plasticity and industry maturity are more likely to be integrated as divisions (subsidiaries) into multidivisional organizations (holding companies) and firms which are characterized by low levels of investment plasticity and industry maturity are more likely to remain independent, multidivisional organizations will, on average, be characterized by higher levels of investment plasticity and industry maturity than ordinary corporations.

Table 2.4 reports the results of the ordered probit routine. The upper part of Table 2.4 contains the values of the log-likelihood function and a restricted log-likelihood function. The latter has been computed assuming that all slopes are zero. The threshold parameters are still allowed to vary freely. The model simply assigns each cell a predicted probability equal to the sample proportion. This appropriately measures the contribution of the level of investment plasticity and industry maturity to the log-likelihood function. Hence, the chi-squared statistic is a valid test statistic for the hypothesis that all slopes on the nonconstant regressors "investment plasticity" and "industry maturity" are zero. This hypothesis cannot be refuted on the basis of the value of the chi-squared statistic.

As documented by the matrix of Table 2.4, neither of the two independent variables can explain the prevailing organizational mode of capital allocation and corporate governance at a statistically acceptable significance level. The second variable, the level of industry maturity, even has a negative sign. The model predicts only fourteen out of thirty-one cases correctly.

The statistical test results support the theory of organizational response to capital market inefficiencies under relational regulation (see Chapter 1). Under relational regulation, multidivisional organizations and holding companies do not possess efficiency advantages over capital markets with regard to capital allocation within mature industries. Nor do multidivisional organizations and holding companies provide superior governance structures for investment relations which are characterized by high levels of industry plasticity. The high degree of ownership concentration within relational capital markets already provides efficient governance structures. At the same time, relational capital markets fail to aggregate and transmit large amounts of scattered knowledge. As a result, unintermediated (and intermediated) relational capital markets cannot allocate scarce capital within immature industries more effectively

Table 2.4 Statistical results for Germany
Ordered Probit Model, Max. Likelihood Estimates
Log - Likelihood = -31.59474; Restricted (slope = 0) Log-L = -32.56179;
Chi-squared (2) = 1.934092; Significance level = 0.3802045

Variable	Coefficient	Std. Error	t-ratio	Prob $\lvert t\rvert \geqslant x$	Mean	Std.Dev.
Constant	1.3433	0.6422	2.093	0.03632		
Investment plasticity	0.13890E-01	0.2561E-01	0.542	0.58753	6.3065	7.3444
Industry maturity	-0.19903	0.1602	-1.242	0.21411	3.7742	1.1750
μ_1	1.3514	0.2998	4.507	0.00001		

Correlation between independent variables = -0.33703; sample size n = 31; number of correct predictions = 14 than holding companies or multidivisional organizations. Summing up: German companies cannot economize on organizational variety.

JAPAN

Regulatory environment

Corporate law   The so-called *kabushiki-kaisha*[81] is the Japanese equivalent of a German AG. A *kabushiki-kaisha* may issue several classes of shares which differ in their contents as to the distribution of profit, interest, surplus assets or the retirement of shares by profits.[82] Shares which carry preference rights regarding the distribution of profits may be issued with or without voting rights.[83] Shares which carry multiple voting rights may not be issued.[84] Regardless of the class of shares, shareholder liability is limited to the value at which shares have been issued.[85]

Every *kabushiki-kaisha* has three organs: its general meeting of shareholders, its directors and board of directors, and its auditors. A general meeting of shareholders must be convened at least once a year.[86] Unless otherwise provided for by the Japanese Commercial Code or by corporate statutes, all resolutions of a general meeting must be adopted by a majority of votes of the shareholders present who hold shares representing more than one-half of total voting rights.[87] According to the Japanese Commercial Code, any alternation of corporate statutes; any transfer of the corporation or important parts thereof; any making, alteration or rescission of contracts for leasing the corporation's business, for giving a mandate to manage such business or for sharing the corporation's profits and losses; any reductions of stated capital; the issue of new shares to persons other than current shareholders; the decision to dissolve the corporation; and acquisition of other companies, requires a two-thirds majority of the votes present at the shareholder meeting which must represent more than one-half of total voting rights.[88]

Directors are appointed at a general meeting of shareholders.[89] Every *kabushiki-kaisha* must have at least three directors.[90] The term of office of the first directors must not exceed one year; the term of office of all consecutive directors must not exceed two years.[91] Directors may be removed from office at any time by a two-thirds majority resolution of a general shareholder meeting at which at least one-half of total voting rights is represented. Directors who are removed from office without due cause during their term of office may claim compensation from the corporation for damages caused by such a removal.[92]

The board of directors administers the affairs of the *kabushiki-kaisha*, usually via delegation of competencies to individual directors, and supervises directors.[93] The following matters, however, cannot be delegated to individual directors, but must be decided by the board of directors: acquisition and disposition of important property; loans of large sums; appointment and dismissal of important corporate executives; and establishment, change or discontinuance of important branches, plants or divisions.[94] Unless severed by corporate statutes, resolutions of the board of directors must be approved by more than half of the directors who are present and who constitute a majority of all directors.[95] A *kabushiki-kaisha* must, by a resolution of the board of directors, appoint a representing director who is usually called president.[96] The president and all other directors must receive a remuneration which is either fixed by corporate statutes or determined by a resolution of the general shareholder meeting.[97]

Auditors examine the execution of duties by directors.[98] To avoid conflicts of interests, an auditor may not at the same time be a director, manager or any other employee of the *kabushiki-kaisha*.[99] Auditors are usually appointed for three years, except for the term of office of the first auditors which is limited to one year.[100] All other regulations regarding the appointment, dismissal and remuneration of auditors are the same as those for directors.[101]

Unlike German and US corporate law, the Japanese Commercial Code contains provisions for a meeting of bondholders. Although the meeting of bondholders is not regarded as an organ of the *kabushiki-kaisha*, it may, with a court's permission, adopt resolutions regarding matters which seriously affect the interests of bondholders.[102] A meeting of bondholders shall be convened by the *kabushiki-kaisha* or its debenture management company.[103] The convening of a bondholder meeting may also be demanded by bondholders who hold at least one-tenth of the total amount of debentures.[104] At the meeting, every bondholder has one vote for each minimum amount of the debentures.[105] All major resolutions of the bondholder meeting, including the postponement of interest or principal payments[106] and the appointment or dismissal of representatives and executors,[107] must be approved by a two-thirds majority of the votes present and representing at least one-half of all votes.[108] Any resolution of the bondholder meeting takes effect upon approval by the court.[109] Unlawful and markedly unfair resolutions are not approved by the court.[110]

Accounting, disclosure and auditing rules   Japanese accounting, disclosure and auditing regulations are based on codified law and on generally accepted accounting principles. Major legal requirements are contained in the Commercial Code (CC) and the Securities and Exchange Law (SEL). The provisions of the CC are primarily creditor-oriented and apply to all *kabushiki-kaisha*. The provisions of the SEL, on the other hand, are primarily shareholder-oriented and apply only to companies raising funds in the capital market. Generally accepted accounting principles which have been established through business practices are promulgated by the Business Accounting Deliberation Council (BADC) of the Ministry of Finance under the title "Financial Accounting Standards for Business Enterprises." These principles provide interpretive guidelines to the previously mentioned laws and govern areas which are not explicitly regulated by codified law. Furthermore, Japanese financial accounting is, in a similar fashion to its German counterpart, heavily influenced by tax considerations.

According to the CC, the directors of a *kabushiki-kaisha* must prepare a balance sheet, an income statement, a business report and a proposal for the disposition of profits and losses.[111] Those reports must be audited by the internal auditors[112] (in case of large corporations by external auditors),[113] must be sent together with the audit report to shareholders,[114] and with exception of the business report, must be approved at the general meeting of shareholders.[115]

Under the provisions of the CC, floating assets,[116] including short-term investments,[117] must be valued according to the lower-of-cost-and-market principle. Fixed assets must be valued at historical costs minus reasonable depreciation.[118] Since the CC contains no further specifications regarding the depreciation of fixed assets, accounting reports which are submitted to shareholders for approval must comply with the depreciation regulations included in the Corporate Tax Law in order to avoid arbitrary depreciation. According to the Corporate Tax Law, intangible fixed assets must be depreciated by using the straight-line method; tangible fixed assets may be depreciated by using the straight-line or the declining balance method. Additional depreciation, such as increased initial depreciation and accelerated depreciation, is permitted by the

Special Taxation Measures Law in order to attain certain accounting policy aims.

The Commercial Code further requires every *kabushiki-kaisha* to create two kinds of statutory reserves: capital surplus reserves and earned surplus reserves. Capital surplus reserves include share premiums and any positive difference resulting from capital reduction or merger.[119] Earned surplus reserves shall be accumulated by adding at least 10 percent of cash dividends every fiscal year until the total amount of earned surplus reserves equals 25 percent of the corporation's capital stock.[120]

Further specifications regarding form and content of accounting reports are codified in the Regulation Concerning Balance Sheet, Profit and Loss Statement, Business Report, and Amended Specifications of *kabushiki-kaisha* (an amended law to the Commercial Code, hereafter referred to as Accounting Report Amendments—ARA). According to the regulations contained in the Amendments, every *kabushiki-kaisha* must, among others, report earnings per share,[121] describe the applied valuation and depreciation methods as well as other significant accounting policies or changes thereof,[122] disclose segmented operating results for each division,[123] explain operating results and changes in financial position for at least the past three years,[124] name the top seven major shareholders including the number of shares held,[125] disclose material facts which have occurred after the settlement of accounts,[126] report transactions involving directors, internal auditors, or dominant shareholders[127] and disclose the amount of remuneration paid to directors and internal auditors.[128]

The Commercial Code and its amended laws do not contain any stipulations regarding the arrangement of assets and liabilities. However, the Financial Accounting Standards for Business Enterprises require arrangement by decreasing liquidity (assets) and increasing maturity (liabilities).[129] After the accounting reports have been approved at the general meeting of shareholders, the directors must publish the balance sheet or its summary, and in case of large companies, the profit and loss account or its summary.[130]

Listed corporations, corporations whose securities are traded on the over-the-counter market and companies which intend to issue securities to the general public are further subjected to the accounting, auditing and disclosure regulations of the SEL. These regulations are divided into requirements for the issuance of securities and requirements for the subsequent trading of securities.

Requirements for the issuance of securities consist of a registration statement filed with the Ministry of Finance and a prospectus furnished directly to the public investor.[131] Requirements for the trading of securities comprise annual securities reports, semi-annual reports and temporary reports.[132] All three reports must be filed with the Ministry of Finance, which offers the reports for public perusal.[133]

The annual securities report must include, among other things, detailed information about the company, its shareholders, directors and internal auditors, its business, the condition of its facilities and business operations, its parent company and subsidiaries (if any) and performance of its shares. The company must also report the condition of its cash flows presented on a comparative basis including the last four half-year periods and the next two half-year periods. The company's corporate statutes, the accounting documents reported to or approved by the general meeting of shareholders, and consolidated financial statements for the last two consolidation periods must be attached to the securities report.[134] All financial documents must be audited by a certified public accountant or an independent accounting corporation.[135]

The financial statements filed with the Ministry of Finance must meet the standards set forth in the Regulation Concerning Terminology, Forms and Method of Preparation of Financial Statements, etc. (hereafter referred to as Financial Statement Regulation—FSR). For example, FSR provisions require a much more detailed classification of assets, liabilities and shareholders' equity; demand, among other things, disclosure of revaluation of assets,[136] assets subject to liens,[137] major assets and debentures denominated in foreign currency,[138] contingent liabilities[139] and net assets per share,[140] and encourage disclosure of sales and cost of sales for major business lines.[141] Unlike US corporations, Japanese *kabushiki-kaisha* do not have to disclose accounting data reflecting inflationary effects and are not obligated to provide comparative financial data from previous periods.

The semi-annual report is basically an abbreviated version of the annual securities report. It consists of an interim balance sheet, interim income statement and explanatory notes. Japanese semi-annual reports contain significantly more information than German semi-annual reports. With regard to investment-relevant information, Japanese semi-annual reports are comparable to the quarterly (10-Q) reports filed by US corporations. Contrary to US provisions for 10-Q reports, however, Japanese semi-annual reports must contain an interim audit report.

Temporary reports are not comparable to 8-K reports. Under Japanese regulations, a temporary report must be filed with the Ministry of Finance when a public offering of securities exceeding ¥100 million is made outside Japan, when the company decides to issue securities exceeding ¥100 million without making a public offering, when a change of the parent company, subsidiaries or major shareholders takes place, or when an important disaster occurs.[142] In October 1988 and April 1989, further events (such as corporate merger, assignment of business, change of information on the going public of shares, etc.) were added to this list in order to enhance temporary disclosure requirements. The temporary report must provide investors with background information on the respective event.

Japanese accounting, auditing and disclosure regulations combine German and US traditions. Creditor-oriented and taxation-dominated accounting under the CC is complemented by shareholder-oriented financial reporting under the SEL. Due to the increasing adoption of US standards, Japanese small investors enjoy information advantages over their German counterparts. Since US standards are only partially adopted, however, the remaining information asymmetries between corporate insiders and small investors are higher in Japan than in the US. For example, Japanese laws do not contain any provisions for the disclosure of quarterly financial data, leaving small investors with a considerable information lag.

Laws against insider trading Insider trading in general and insider trading in relation with tender offers in particular have been restricted in Japan since 1989.[143] According to the SEL, insiders must refrain from trading on the basis of unpublished material event information. Insiders who violate these restrictions may be fined up to ¥500,000 or imprisoned for up to six months (in special cases up to ¥3 million or three years' imprisonment).[144] In order to facilitate law enforcement and to enhance market transparency, Japanese regulations oblige shareholders who own more than 10 percent of a listed corporation's outstanding stock and all officers of listed corporations to report their transactions in corporate securities to the Ministry of Finance.[145] In addition, any person who owns more than 5 percent of the outstanding shares of a listed *kabushiki-kaisha* must file with the Ministry of Finance a report detailing his

137

or her shareholdings.[146] This report must be sent to the issuer and to all exchanges at which the shares are listed. Subsequent reports must be filed whenever a material event, such as a change in shareholdings exceeding 1 percent (of all outstanding shares), occurs.[147] Due to these supportive disclosure rules, insider regulations can be enforced more effectively in Japan than in Germany, whose corporate insiders enjoy more anonymity. However, Japanese law enforcement has not yet reached US standards, mainly because the relatively short history of Japanese insider regulation precludes regulatory institutions from acquiring sufficient enforcement experience.

Laws against market manipulation   Japanese regulations protect investors against market manipulation. The SEL prohibits the use of fraudulent devices such as false quotations, misleading rumors, wash sales, matched orders, etc., to induce the purchase or sale of securities.[148] Price stabilization operations are limited to public offerings and secondary distributions of securities.[149] A securities company which executes a stabilization operation must file a prior notification and a subsequent report with the Ministry of Finance. The SEL further prohibits short sales and the placement of orders to buy (or sell) securities as soon as their quotation exceeds (or falls below) a certain price limit.[150]

(Anti-) takeover regulation   Japanese takeover regulations increase the cost of tender offers by imposing various disclosure obligations on bidders and by enhancing the right of target shareholders. Under Japanese law, tender offers cannot be submitted without public disclosure of the offer, notification of the Ministry of Finance and informing of the target company.[151] The bid must remain open for at least twenty and no more than sixty days.[152] During this period the bidder may not acquire any shares without resorting to the offer.[153] Target shareholders are protected against price cuts and price discrimination. Once offered, an increase in the buying price becomes effective for all shares tendered, even those which were tendered prior to the price increase.[154] Japanese takeover regulations further entitle shareholders to withdraw their agreement to tender during the entire period of the tender offer.[155] If more than the specified number of shares has been tendered, bidders must buy shares on a pro rata rather than a first-come-first-served basis.[156] Contrary to the US and similar to Germany, hostile takeovers have never been a big issue in Japan. Consequently, Japanese legislators have not come under political pressure to enact anti-takeover laws.

Diversification requirements Japanese financial intermediaries are subjected to diversification requirements. Investment trusts[157] and insurance companies (including private pension funds) may not acquire more than 10 percent of a single corporation's outstanding shares.[158] In addition, insurance companies may not invest more than 30 percent of their assets into stock and may not invest more than 10 percent of their assets into securities of a single corporation.[159] All other financial intermediaries, including commercial and investment banks, may not acquire more than 5 percent of a single corporation's outstanding stock.[160] Since Japan's system is similar to the German model, private pension funds are of minor importance. However, the assets accumulated by private pension funds have steadily increased during recent decades.

Bank regulation Universal banking is prohibited under Japanese regulations. According to the Japanese SEL, commercial and trust banks may not engage in investment banking activities such as securities dealing, securities brokerage, underwriting, distribution or public offering of securities.[161] In addition, bank directors may not simultaneously serve as directors of other companies without authorization from the Ministry of Finance.[162]

Under Japanese law, commercial banks are entitled to acquire equity stakes in non-banks. However, no bank may acquire more than 5 percent of a *kabushiki-kaisha*'s outstanding equity. As a result, Japanese banks are less strictly regulated than US banks but do not enjoy the same latitude as German universal banks.

Prohibition of holding companies A specific feature of Japanese regulations is the categorical prohibition of holding companies. Under Japanese law it is forbidden to establish a company whose principal objective is to control the business activities of other companies through majority stockholdings.[163]

Conclusion Japan's current regulatory environment may be characterized as hybrid with neoclassical and relational elements. Unlike Germany, Japan underwent fundamental regulatory changes after World War II. The majority of relational regulations which had been established during the Meiji and prewar era have been superseded by neoclassical regulations in the postwar period. In addition, some of the relational elements which have survived, such as the accounting, disclosure and auditing rules contained in the Commercial Code, were offset in their effect on capital allocation and corporate governance by the introduction of additional neoclassical requirements.

However, several relational elements withstood the general shift toward neoclassical regulation. The most important of these elements is the right of commercial and trust banks to acquire equity holdings in non-banks. Although this right is restricted by the 5 percent rule, it opens the door to extensive long-term investment and governance relationships between deposit-taking banks and nonfinancial enterprises.

Furthermore, the relational history of Japan's regulatory environment has led to a "relational interpretation" of neoclassical law. As a result there are various discrepancies between codified law and legal reality (see for example Henderson 1991; Baum and Schaede 1994).

Japan's capital market in comparison

The separation of commercial and investment banking guarantees a relatively well-developed equity market. The relative strength of the Japanese stock market is documented in Table 2.1 (see above). At the end of 1994 there were 1,689 domestic *kabushiki-kaisha* listed on the first and second section of the Tokyo Stock Exchange (TSE). The total number of domestic *kabushiki-kaisha* listed on at least one of Japan's eight stock exchanges (Tokyo, Osaka, Nagoya, Kyoto, Hiroshima, Fukuoka, Niigata and Sapporo) amounts to over 2,000. According to the Japan Securities Research Institute (1994: 158, Table 3), there were a total of 2,118 listed Japanese *kabushiki-kaisha* at the end of 1992. Adjusted market capitalization of all domestic *kabushiki-kaisha* listed on the first or second section of the TSE reached 27.1 percent of Japan's GDP in 1994. In this respect, the TSE clearly outperforms all German exchanges combined (4.1 percent), but remains well below the combined size of the New York Stock Exchange and NASDAQ (70.3 percent).

The nominal value of outstanding bonds as a percentage of GDP is larger in Japan (93.4) than in the US (87.4) and Germany (44.7). Private nonfinancial enterprises account for 9.8 percent of all outstanding bonds in Japan, compared to 21.3 percent in the US and 0.1 percent in Germany. The debt-equity ratio of all Japanese *kabushiki-kaisha* averages 3.98, compared to 0.87 for US corporations and 2.83 for listed German AGs and KGaAs.

These data reflect the specifics of Japan's hybrid capital market regulation. The relational elements of Japan's regulatory environment guarantee a strong and well developed stock market. The combination of relational (equity holdings by banks) and neoclassical (separation of commercial and investment banking) bank regulations enables banks to reduce the default risk of their loans to non-banks without giving banks excessive control over non-banks.[164] As a result, Japanese non-banks avoid credit rationing[165] and at the same time enjoy fairly unlimited access to strong capital markets. Empirical evidence confirms that the cost of corporate capital is significantly lower in Japan than in the US (Friend and Tokutsu 1987; Ando and Auerbach 1988).

Structure and concentration of corporate ownership

The relational elements of Japan's regulatory environment discourage ownership concentration by individual investors and restrict ownership concentration by financial intermediaries. Commercial and trust banks may not acquire more than 5 percent, and insurance companies and investment trusts may not acquire more than 10 percent of any *kabushiki-kaisha*'s outstanding equity. Holding companies are categorically prohibited.

Despite these restrictions, Japan's level of ownership intermediation exceeds that of Germany. As shown in Table 2.2 above, ownership intermediation amounts to 68.6 percent in Japan compared to 64 percent in Germany and 43.8 percent in the US. However, the relatively high level of ownership intermediation does not result in a high level of ownership concentration. As Table 2.3 (above) documents, the Japanese level of ownership concentration is similar to the US level and differs substantially from Germany's high level of ownership concentration.

The comparatively low level of ownership concentration may be regarded as an indicator for, first, capital misallocation within industries which are characterized by medium-to-high levels of industry maturity, and second, severe governance problems within Japanese *kabushiki-kaisha* which are characterized by medium-to-high levels of investment plasticity. Considering the prohibition of holding companies, one might be even more inclined to accept this interpretation; however, it is innaccurate. The discrepancy between

Japan's level of ownership intermediation and Japan's level of ownership concentration is caused by financial keiretsu.

Currently, there are eight financial keiretsu in Japan. They are classified into two size categories: the six major financial keiretsu and the two of medium size. The six major keiretsu include Mitsui, Mitsubishi, Sumitomo, Sanwa, Dai-Ichi Kangin (DKB) and Fuyo. Mitsui, Mitsubishi and Sumitomo are contemporary descendants of former zaibatsu—large, partly monopolistic holding companies which were dissolved by US occupation forces after World War II. The two medium-sized financial keiretsu, Tokai and Industrial Bank of Japan, are of less overall economic importance than the six major groups. In 1993 the six major financial keiretsu accounted for 3.79 percent of employees, 11.89 percent of assets, 13.27 percent of sales and 23.82 percent of net profits in Japan's company sector (Toyo Keizai Shinpo Sha 1995: 24–7).

As discussed in Chapter 1 above, financial keiretsu are based on cross shareholdings, personal ties, keiretsu-internal lending, keiretsu-internal trading and informal communication. Although keiretsu-internal cross shareholdings are usually small on a bilateral basis, they become substantial when aggregated over the entire keiretsu. Table 2.5 reports empirical data on aggregated cross shareholdings and additional governance mechanisms within Japan's six major financial keiretsu.

From the viewpoint of capital allocation and corporate governance, financial keiretsu are a perfect substitute for holding companies. As a delegated monitor on behalf of the entire keiretsu, the main bank exercises approximately the same amount of control over each member corporation as the headquarters of a holding company exercises over each subsidiary. Due to the wide variety of supportive governance mechanisms (internal lending, internal trading, personal ties, informal communication) financial keiretsu achieve the same level of corporate control with a lower level of equity ownership than holding companies.[166]

Organizational response

The Japanese-specific efficiency match between relevant characteristics of an investment relation and alternative organizational modes of capital allocation and corporate governance is shown in Figure 2.1.

As a result of the relational regulatory elements, the Japanese capital market is able to aggregate large amounts of scattered

Table 2.5 Cross shareholdings, internal lending, internal trading and personal ties within Japan's six major financial keiretsu (1993/94)

	Mitsui	Mitsubishi	Sumitomo	Sanwa	Dai-Ichi Kangin	Fuyo
Presidents' club	Nimokukai	Kinyokai	Hakusuikai	Sansuikai	Sankinkai	Fuyokai
Member corporations (No.)	25	27	19	42	45	28
Percentage of outstanding shares of member corporations held by other member corporations	16.77	26.11	24.45	16.41	11.92	14.90
Internal lending as a percentage of total debt	20.36	21.73	20.77	17.25	16.29	16.57
Percentage of member corporations with at least one director sent by another member corporation	35	100	50	70	57	48
Purchases of member corporations from the keiretsu's general trading firm(s) (as a percentage of total purchases)	2.8	9.6	7.6	2.3	2.9	2.6
Sales of member corporations to the keiretsu's general trading firm(s) (as a percentage of total sales)	5.9	17.8	27.3	2.7	4.8	7.6

Sources: Toyo Keizai Shinpo Sha (1995); Fair Trade Commission of Japan; Dodwell Marketing Consultants (1994)

knowledge in order to allocate scarce capital to high-yield uses within immature industries. The competitiveness of Japan's information and telecommunications industries as well as its biotechnology industries supports this conclusion. Japan's regulatory environment further enables small investors to efficiently govern corporate investments as long as the associated degree of investment plasticity remains at low levels. Once the degrees of investment plasticity and industry maturity reach medium levels, the Japanese capital market will experience serious allocation and governance problems. In these cases, investment efficiency can be maintained through keiretsu organization. Financial keiretsu provide adequate governance (allocation) mechanisms for investment relations whose degree of investment plasticity (maturity) exceeds low levels but does not yet reach high levels. Since keiretsu organization provides the same level of corporate governance as

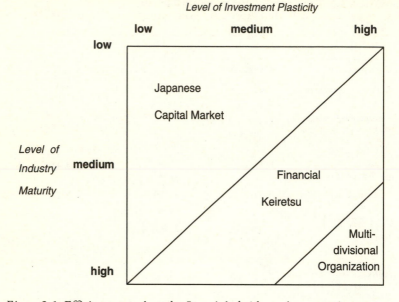

Figure 2.1 Efficiency match under Japan's hybrid regulatory environment

holding companies at a lower level of ownership concentration, financial keiretsu outperform capital markets at lower levels of investment plasticity and industry maturity than holding companies. Compared to financial keiretsu, holding companies have to sacrifice larger amounts of scattered knowledge in order to achieve governance efficiency. Like holding companies, financial keiretsu are capable of adjusting ownership concentration to increasing levels of investment plasticity and industry maturity.

Once investment plasticity and industry maturity reach high levels, however, financial keiretsu will be outperformed by multidivisional organizations. Unlike financial keiretsu, multidivisional organizations have access to an internal control apparatus and are able to reallocate cash flows in a real-time fashion. Cash flows are not automatically reinvested at the source division, but may be instantly transferred to other divisions.

Statistical test

Basically, the same statistical model which has been employed to test the theory of organizational response to capital market inefficiencies under Germany's relational regulation (see above) is used to test the theory of organizational response to capital market inefficiencies under Japan's hybrid regulatory environment. Except for MODE 1, which now represents financial keiretsu instead of holding companies, all variables and equations remain unchanged. Contrary to the German case, however, empirical evidence from Japan would support the tested theory if a statistically significant correlation between the underlying levels of industry maturity and investment plasticity on the one hand, and the prevailing organizational mode of capital allocation and corporate governance on the other, exists, i.e. if a statistically significant number of multidivisional organizations (financial keiretsu) prevails as a response to capital market inefficiencies in case of high (medium) levels of industry maturity and investment plasticity.

Statistical results

The statistical results for Japan are based on a random sample of n = 50 *kabushiki-kaisha* out of all nonfinancial *kabushiki-kaisha* listed on the first sections of the Tokyo, Osaka and Nagoya stock exchanges. The Japanese sample is larger than the German sample because of the larger number of listed *kabushiki-kaisha* in comparison to listed AGs and KGaAs. The necessary data have been obtained through interviews and the analysis of corporate reports and other corporate publications. Appendix B of this book lists the names of all corporations included in the sample.

Kabushiki-kaisha which belong to the Nimoku-kai (Mitsui), Kinyo-kai (Mitsubishi), Hakusui-kai (Sumitomo), Sansui-kai (Sanwa), Sankin-kai (Dai-Ichi Kangin), Fuyo-kai (Fuyo) or Satsuki-kai (Tokai) were classified as keiretsu-organizations (MODE$_i$ = 1). The classification and statistical treatment of multidivisional organizations does not differ from the method applied in the German model (see above).

Table 2.6 reports the statistical results of the ordered probit routine. The chi-squared statistic refutes the hypothesis that all slopes on the nonconstant regressors (investment plasticity, industry maturity) are zero. This refutation is statistically significant at the 99 percent level.

The coefficients of both independent variables have the theoretically predicted sign (positive). The effect of the first independent variable (investment plasticity) is statistically significant at the

Table 2.6 Statistical results for Japan
Ordered Probit Model, Max. Likelihood Estimates
Log - Likelihood = -44.57120; Restricted (slope = 0) Log-L = -51.09568;
Chi-squared (2) = 13.04896; Significance level = 0.1467084E-02

Variable	Coefficient	Std. Error	t-ratio	Prob $|t| \geqslant x$	Mean	Std.Dev.
Constant	-2.1135	0.9073	-2.329	0.01983		
Investment plasticity	0.72608E-01	0.2264E-01	3.207	0.00134	6.6440	7.0764
Industry maturity	0.53743	0.2159	2.490	0.01279	3.3800	1.2599
μ_1	0.48568	0.1600	3.035	0.00240		

Correlation between independent variables = -0.32673; sample size n = 50; number of correct predictions = 31

99 percent level. The effect of the second independent variable is statistically significant at the 95 percent level. The two independent variables are not highly correlated. The model correctly predicted thirty-one out of fifty cases.

These statistical results support the theory of organizational response to capital market inefficiencies under Japan's hybrid capital market regulation. Financial keiretsu and multidivisional organizations are an efficient response to the allocation and governance problems associated with medium and high levels of industry maturity and investment plasticity.

UNITED STATES

Regulatory environment

Corporate law While German and Japanese corporate law falls under federal legislature and is predominantly restrictive, US corporate law falls under state legislature and is predominately permissive. As a result, rights and obligations are less uniformly allocated in US than in German and Japanese corporations. For example, financial innovations, which are supported by many state corporate statutes in the US, have resulted in a wide variety of different classes of shares. Each class of shares carries specific voting and/or dividend rights.

Since over one-third of all domestic corporations listed on the NYSE are incorporated in the small state of Delaware, the Delaware Legislature and Delaware Supreme Court are important sources of corporate law in the US. Another major source of corporate law is the Models Business Corporation Act (MBCA), developed in 1950 by a committee of the American Bar Association. In 1984 a new version of the MBCA, the so-called Revised MBCA (RMBCA), was introduced. Both the original MBCA and the new RMBCA have influenced state incorporation statutes in more than twenty-five states. The RMBCA and the Delaware statute are primarily permissive rather than restrictive. Although most states have followed the trend toward flexible statutes, some (e.g. California) have retained substantive regulations.

US corporations are divided into two categories: closely held and publicly held corporations. Closely held corporations are comparable to German GmbHs, German non-listed AGs and Japanese non-listed *kabushiki-kaisha*. Typically, there is no outside market for shares of a closely held corporation and transfer of shares is restricted. In most cases shareholders of closely held corporations participate in management.

Publicly held corporations are comparable to listed AGs and listed *kabushiki-kaisha*. Publicly held corporations have registered a public distribution of their securities under Section 12 of the Securities Exchange Act of 1934. Usually shareholders of publicly held corporations do not participate in corporate management. Separation of ownership and control prevails within publicly held corporations.

State corporation statutes, corporate charters and corporate bylaws distribute corporate powers among shareholders, directors and officers. Shareholders are the ultimate owners of the corporation, but have only limited powers to participate in corporate management and control. Differences among state corporation statutes notwithstanding, US shareholders enjoy limited liability;[167] have the right to receive a proportion of dividends as they are declared;[168] and are entitled to elect and dismiss directors,[169] to approve or disapprove proposed amendments to the articles of incorporation,[170] and to approve or disapprove other fundamental changes such as mergers,[171] compulsory share exchanges,[172] dissolution[173] and disposition of large amounts of corporate property.[174] Unlike German shareholders, US shareholders are entitled by many states to remove directors without cause,[175] to inspect corporate books and records[176] and to file derivative suits on behalf of the corporation.[177]

Shareholders cast their votes at annual, or, if necessary, special meetings.[178] Each shareholder may vote in person or by proxy.[179] Unless the articles of incorporation or bylaws stipulate otherwise,

147

measures will be approved by majority.[180] Currently, all states allow corporations to increase the percentage of votes which are required to approve a measure or elect directors to any desired number.

The business and affairs of US corporations are managed by the board of directors. According to Section 8.01(b) of the RMBCA, "all corporate powers shall be exercised by or under the authority of, and the business and affairs of the corporation shall be managed under the direction of its board of directors, subject to any limitation set forth in the articles of incorporation." Important directoral functions include the declaration of dividends,[181] the valuation and issuance of corporate stock,[182] the valuation of property and services received for stock,[183] approval of stock repurchases[184] and the appointment and dismissal of officers.[185] When performing these functions, directors act in fiduciary capacity.[186]

The entire board of directors may stand for re-election every year. If permitted by state corporation law, the articles of incorporation may provide for a "staggered" or "classified" board. In this case, the board is divided into two or three groups, each of which serves for two (or three) years. Each year another group is elected.[187]

Corporate officers administer the day-to-day affairs of the corporation and are subject to the control and direction of the board of directors. Since the officers of a corporation are its agents, their powers are controlled by the laws of agency.[188] Most states require that a corporation has at least four officers: president, at least one vice-president, treasurer and secretary. In closely held corporations, all officers are usually board members (inside directors), whereas officers of public corporations may or may not be board members.

Accounting, disclosure and auditing rules Following the tradition of English law, US accounting standards are not based on codified law, but rely on Generally Accepted Accounting Principles (GAAP) developed by the accounting profession. These principles are predominately shareholder-oriented and are independent of tax considerations. Compared to German and Japanese provisions, US accounting standards and disclosure requirements differ with regard to form, substance and frequency of financial reports. Contrary to German provisions which require assets and liabilities to be arranged in order of increasing liquidity on the balance sheet, US standards require arrangement by decreasing liquidity order. Major valuation differences compared to the German or Japanese accounting system include the valuation of short-term investments at market value,[189] the recognition of revenues and profits according to the percentage-of-completion method in case of long-term construction contracts[190] and the valuation of long-term equity investments between 20 percent and 50 percent of the investor's outstanding voting shares according to the equity method.[191] All other assets must be valued in accordance with the lower-of-cost-and-market (fair) value principle.[192] Long-lived assets must be recorded as historical costs and are depreciated in straight-line or by accelerated methods.[193] Excess depreciation for tax purposes is not allowed in financial statements. Differences between financial and tax depreciation must be reported as deferred taxes.[194] Unlike German AGs, KGaAs and GmbHs, US corporations are obliged to report earnings per share[195] and changes in shareholder equity.[196] Under current GAAP, the latter explicitly includes (besides retained earnings, dividends, etc.) unrealized gains or losses on short-term investments[197] and accumulated gains or losses on translation of foreign-currency-denominated financial statements (in case of consolidated accounts).[198]

Major differences between US accounting standards and German as well as Japanese provisions exist furthermore with regard to segment reporting and inflation accounting. In addition to the disclosure of information about specific industries and foreign operations,[199] US companies must report the amount of sales to major customers.[200] To inform investors about the consequence of inflation, large companies must disclose supplementary accounting data based on current cost valuations.[201] Consolidation requirements, on the other hand, do not differ substantially among the three countries.

US corporations which have issued or plan to issue securities to the general public are subject to the extensive disclosure requirements contained in the Securities Act of 1933 and the Securities Exchange Act of 1934. According to the Securities Act, securities may not be offered to the public unless they have been registered with the Securities Exchange Commission (SEC). The registration application has to be submitted to the SEC by using one of their registration forms. The most common are Forms S-1, S-2 and S-3. S-1 is the most comprehensive registration statement; S-2 and S-3 are abbreviated versions for present and established registrants respectively.

Form S-1 consists of the basic information package for annual reports, details on the offering and information about the company's directors and officers. The basic information package for annual

149

reports is composed of a business description, stock price and dividend information regarding the last two years, selected financial data (including five-year trend data), management's discussion and analysis of financial condition and results of operations, and audited financial statements with supplementary notes (including income and cash flow statements for the last three years and balance sheets for the last two years).

Section 13 of the Securities Exchange Act of 1934 requires publicly held corporations to update the original statements through subsequent disclosures.[202] These update reports must be filed on Forms 10-K, 10-Q and 8-K. 10-K contains the basic information package for annual reports and additional information such as schedules detailing selected asset and liability accounts, management remuneration and transactions, and security ownership of directors, chief executives and major shareholders. Form 10-Q is the quarterly report to the SEC. Basically, it includes unaudited financial statements for the respective quarter, accumulative statements starting from the beginning of the fiscal period, comparative statements from the equivalent quarter of the previous fiscal year and an update on major changes and developments since the end of the last quarter. Form 8-K must be filed to disclose unscheduled material events within fifteen days of their occurrence.

The Securities Exchange Act also defines the disclosure requirements in connection with proxy solicitations. According to Rule 14a-3, proxy solicitations must contain a full discussion of the matters to be voted on and must be accompanied by an annual report if the present management is making the solicitation for a meeting at which directors are to be elected.[203] In most states this rule is the only legal basis to require the distribution of annual reports. Since the information disclosed in accordance with Form 10-K includes and exceeds the information contained in annual reports, publicly held corporations usually distribute annual reports to shareholders even if management does not make any solicitation.

The described disclosure regulations are backed by a variety of enforcement devices. Both the Securities Act of 1933 and the Securities Exchange Act of 1934 provide criminal penalties for wilful material false or misleading statements. The SEC is empowered to suspend or withdraw registrations which do not comply with legal provisions.

Summing up, US accounting standards and auditing and disclosure requirements effectively reduce information asymmetries between corporate insiders and outsiders. Based on the disclosed information, even small investors can easily discover a corporation's current financial and economic situation. Hidden reserves are hard to create by management and easy to detect by investors.

Laws against insider trading   Under US regulations small investors are effectively protected against insider trading. Rule 10b-5 of the Securities Exchange Act prohibits security trading on the basis of unpublished material information.[204] Insiders must either disclose their material information or refrain from trading. If detected, insider trading may be sanctioned by several years of imprisonment. Section 16 of the Securities Exchange Act requires corporate insiders, defined as officers, directors and all owners of at least 10 percent of a class of equity securities, to periodically file statements showing all their equity holdings.[205] Corporate insiders must further report their purchases and sales of equity securities. All short-swing profits, i.e. profits which result from purchase and sale within less than six months, are fully recoverable by the corporation (even if the profits did not result from inside information).[206] Failure to report insider holdings and transactions leads to criminal sanctions.

Laws against market manipulation   Sections 9 and 10 of the 1934 Act prohibit certain kinds of market manipulation and subject others to SEC regulation.[207] Strictly prohibited are wash sales and matched orders for the purpose of conveying false or misleading market characteristics; consecutive transactions in which the price of a security is deliberately increased or decreased or in which active trading is imitated in an effort to encourage transactions by others; material false and misleading statements by brokers, dealers, sellers and buyers; and the circulation of information about market operations conducted to affect prices. Stop loss orders and short sales are among those practices which are subjected to SEC regulation. On the other hand, efforts which are limited to stabilizing the offer price as part of the underwriting services are specifically permitted.

(Anti-) takeover regulation   Until the mid-1980s takeover regulation was considered a federal domain. The Williams Act of 1968 was interpreted as preemptive federal regulation which precluded states from passing individual takeover laws. The Williams Act is moderately anti-takeover. It increases the cost of cash tender offers by requiring bidders for publicly held corporations to refrain from giving false, misleading or incomplete statements[208] and to disclose the source of funds for their offer, the purpose of their offer and any contracts or understandings with respect to the corporation.[209] Moreover, the act permits shareholders to withdraw deposited securities within seven days of an offer,[210] mandates the bidder to purchase on a pro rata basis if more shares than the bidder specified have been tendered,[211] and requires the bidder to pay any increase in the offer price to all tendering shareholders, even those who tendered before the price increase.[212] SEC filing and public disclosure requirements are also imposed on issuers making an offer for their own shares and everyone who acquires at least 5 percent of any class of shares of a publicly held corporation.[213]

In 1987 the Supreme Court opened the door to a series of state anti-takeover laws by rejecting the argument that state anti-takeover regulations are preempted by the Williams Act.[214] Since the Supreme Court's ruling more than forty states[215] have adopted anti-takeover statutes which are designed to further increase the cost of hostile takeovers. The regulatory spectrum ranges from facilitating takeover litigation to validating poison pills.[216] State anti-takeover regulations complement federal diversification requirements and prohibition of universal banking in an effort to disperse corporate ownership.

Diversification requirements According to the Investment Company Act of 1940, a mutual fund wanting to advertise itself as diversified must comply with the following restrictions affecting 75 percent of its assets. First, the mutual fund may not use any of these restricted three-quarters of its assets to acquire more than 10 percent of a company's outstanding stock. Second, of this 75 percent no more than 5 percent may be invested in the securities of any one issuer.[217]

These requirements do not prevent a mutual fund from gaining corporate control by investing the unrestricted part of its portfolio (25 percent) in a single company's stock, or by choosing not to call itself diversified and consequently be free of any restrictions. However, additional regulations apply. If an investment company owned 5 percent of a corporation's stock or sat on its board, the corporation would become a statutory affiliate of the investment company and its principal underwriter.[218] This would automatically trigger insider restrictions. Moreover, a buyout, exchange of shares, conversion of shares or sale of shares by the corporation to the investment company would require SEC exemption. Without SEC exemption the investment company would also be unable to exert joint control with another financial institution. Even investment companies which own less than 5 percent of a corporation's outstanding stock need prior SEC approval if they want to exercise joint control with an affiliate.[219] Subchapter M of the Internal Revenue Code allows diversified mutual funds to pass income (capital gains, dividends) untaxed on to shareholders. To be regarded as diversified under tax law, a mutual fund must not, for half of its portfolio, invest more than 5 percent in a single corporation or acquire more than 10 percent of the securities of a single issuer.[220] Although these regulations do not prohibit investment companies from holding large blocks of a corporation's outstanding shares, they significantly increase the cost of ownership concentration.

Insurance companies, which are regulated by state laws, are usually precluded from exercising control over non-insurers. In addition, most life insurance companies must comply with strict diversification provisions. For example, in the state of New York, traditionally home of many insurance firms, life insurance companies may not invest more than 2 percent of their assets in a single corporation and may not invest more than 20 percent of their assets or one-half of their surplus in stock.[221]

Pension funds are regulated at the federal level by the Employment Retirement Income Security Act of 1974 (ERISA). The Act requires reasonable diversification and prohibits pension funds from investing more than 10 percent of their assets into securities of the employer.[222] ERISA further mandates fiduciary responsibility for those managing the pension plan and its assets. Plan operators must act with care, skill, prudence and diligence.[223] These provisions force pension fund managers to adopt passive and low-risk investment strategies. A popular way to comply with fiduciary duties is to imitate the investment strategies of other pension fund managers.

Bank regulation   Legal restrictions have historically kept US banks from expanding and gaining non-default control over non-banks. The National Bank Act of 1863 confined national banks to a single location. The McFadden Act of 1927 allowed national banks to branch within a city or town and later within an entire state, but only if permitted by state law.[224] The Glass-Steagall Act of 1933 severed commercial banking from investment banking.[225] Commercial banks were prevented from continuing to avoid the direct prohibition on stock dealing by owning, underwriting, selling or distributing securities through their affiliates, while investment banks were prohibited from receiving deposits and granting loans like commercial banks.

Bank trust departments remained commercial banks' only direct link to non-default decision rights over non-banks. However, diversification requirements limit the amount of control which commercial banks can exercise over non-banks through their trust departments. Bank trust funds may not invest more than 10 percent of their assets in the stock of any single corporation.[226]

Bank holding companies are commercial banks' only indirect link to non-default decision rights over non-banks. Bank holding companies emerged as a response to the restrictions on branching and interstate banking. In the 1950s US banks began to evade branching restrictions by founding holding companies and chaining banks together as separately incorporated subsidiaries. But interstate banking remained almost entirely prohibited by the "Douglas Amendment" to the Bank Holding Company Act of 1956.[227] With respect to equity holdings, bank holding companies are not as stringently regulated as their bank subsidiaries. Bank holding companies may own stock. The Bank Holding Company Act of 1956, however, restricts stock ownership of non-banks by bank holding companies to passive ownership of no more than 5 percent of the voting stock of any non-banking corporation.[228] In addition, subordination rules which place influential creditors at a disadvantage in case of bankruptcy have caused banks to think twice before acquiring minority holdings in non-banks. Although the restrictions on interstate banking and the stringent separation of commercial and investment banking have recently begun to erode, the structure of the US banking sector still reflects the neoclassical tradition of bank regulation.

Conclusion US capital market regulations represent the prototype of neoclassical regulation. All regulations are intended to enhance competition and to strengthen market forces. The separation of commercial and investment banking guarantees an innovative and highly competitive investment sector. Even smaller corporations have direct access to a well-developed capital market. Small investors benefit from extensive and strictly enforced accounting, disclosure and auditing rules, tough insider restrictions and well-enforced prohibitions of market manipulation.

Financial intermediaries are effectively precluded from acquiring majority control over nonfinancial corporations. Banks have historically been kept small and weak through branching restrictions, the separation of commercial and investment banking and restrictions on equity ownership. Investment companies, insurance companies and pension funds are subjected to strict diversification requirements. These regulations result in the neoclassical ideal of fragmented corporate ownership.[229]

The US capital market in comparison

The US capital market is the largest in the world. As reported in Table 2.1 above, 6,923 domestic corporations were listed at the NYSE and NASDAQ at the end of 1994. Adjusted market capitalization of these corporations amounted to $4,737.7 billion or 70.3 percent of the US GDP.

The nominal value of outstanding bonds amounted to $5,885.4 billion or 87.4 percent of the US GDP at year-end 1994. Government and government agencies accounted for 58.9 percent of all outstanding bonds. Private nonfinancial enterprises are the second largest debtor with a share of 21.3 percent. This relatively high percentage suggests that it is easier for US nonfinancial corporations to issue bonds than for Japanese nonfinancial *kabushiki-kaisha* (9.8 percent) or German nonfinancial AGs and KGaAs (0.1 percent). Contrary to Germany and similar to Japan, private financial enterprises do not dominate the bond market in the US. They accounted for 16.1 percent of all outstanding bonds at year-end 1994, compared to 18.0 percent in Japan and 47.7 percent in Germany. This relatively low percentage suggests that bank intermediation is of less importance in the US than in Germany.

The average debt-equity ratio of domestic nonfinancial corporations is at 0.87, far below the debt-equity ratios of their German (2.83) and Japanese (3.98) counterparts. The low debt-equity ratios of US corporations reflects the strength of the US equity market, the weakness of US commercial banks and the severity of credit rationing. Unlike German universal banks and Japanese city and trust banks, US commercial banks cannot exercise non-default control over their corporate customers. Consequently, US banks are not able to control the default risk of corporate loans in the same way as their German and Japanese counterparts. As a result, US corporations are subjected to credit rationing.

Structure and concentration of corporate ownership

US neoclassical capital market regulations restrict ownership intermediation and ownership concentration. As shown in Table 2.2 above, private households comprise the largest group of shareholders, owning 49.8 percent of all outstanding stock. Pension funds are the second largest group, owning 29.2 percent of corporate equities. Banks hold only 0.3 percent. The Flow of Funds Tables do not report shareholdings by nonfinancial enterprises. Since US corporations do not form large industrial groups based on majority ownership or cross-shareholdings (see Kester 1992), ownership intermediation by nonfinancial enterprises is of less importance in the US than in Germany (Japan) where nonfinancial enterprises as a group own 42 percent (23.8 percent) of the outstanding shares of all listed domestic corporations.

As a result of neoclassical capital market regulations, corporate ownership is highly fragmented in the United States. As reported in Table 2.3 above, only 3.6 percent of all domestic corporations included in the S&P 500, S&P MidCap 400 and S&P SmallCap 600 have a majority shareholder who controls at least 50 percent of the voting rights. In comparison, 73.2 percent of Germany's 550 largest listed AGs and KGaAs have a majority shareholder.

Organizational response

According to the theory developed in Chapter 1, neoclassical capital markets are an efficient form of allocating scarce capital within immature industries. The international competitiveness of the US biotechnology, telecommunications, entertainment and financial services industries supports this hypothesis. In addition, neoclassical capital markets are an efficient mode of governing investment relations whose level of investment plasticity remains at low-to-medium levels.

In case of medium-to-high levels of industry maturity and investment plasticity, holding companies and multidivisional organizations are efficient organizational responses to the resulting capital market inefficiencies. Although bank holding companies are entitled under US law to acquire up to 5 percent of the outstanding

Table 2.7 Assets of six largest German, Japanese and US banks ($ billion)

German banks[a]		Japanese banks[a]		US banks[b]	
Deutsche Bank	370.0	Tokyo Mitsubishi B.[d]	722.7	Chase Manhattan[e]	308.0
Dresdner Bank	258.4	Sakura Bank	526.4	Citicorp.	257.5
Westdeutsche LB[c]	244.4	Sumitomo Bank	524.2	BankAmerica	229.9
Commerzbank	220.9	Dai-Ichi Kangyo Bank	524.0	NationsBank	182.1
Bayer. Vereinsbank	205.4	Sanwa Bank	520.3	J.P. Morgan	178.3
Bayer. Hypobank	177.8	Fuji Bank	508.9	First Chicago (NBD)	124.2
Total	1476.9	Total	2802.5	Total	1280.0
Total as % of GDP	34.0	Total as % of GDP	59.5	Total as % of GDP	18.0

a 1994
b third quarter 1995
c the Westdeutsche Landesbank is a state-owned bank of Germany's largest state North
   Rhine-Westphalia
d the Bank of Tokyo (total assets: 233.4) and the Mitsubishi Bank (total assets: 489.3) are
   scheduled to merge in April 1996 to form the Tokyo Mitsubishi Bank
e Chemical Bank (total assets: 187.9) and Chase Manhattan (total assets: 120.1) have agreed:
   to merge under the name Chase Manhattan in 1996

Sources: corporate annual reports, OECD main economic indicators, *Federal Reserve Bulletin*, own calculations

equity of non-banks, financial keiretsu are unlikely to emerge within the US regulatory environment. Unlike Japanese banks, US banks have traditionally been precluded from exercising non-default control over non-banks. Branching restrictions and the Glass-Steagall Act have kept US banks small and weak compared to their Japanese and German counterparts. Table 2.7 compares the size of the six largest German, Japanese and US banks. Although Table 2.7 is based on 1995 data for the US and 1994 data for Germany and Japan, the differences in size are significant. Total assets of the six largest US banks amount to 18.0 percent of the US GDP, while total assets of the six largest German (Japanese) banks amount to 34.0 percent (59.5 percent) of Germany's (Japan's) GDP.

Contrary to Japanese banks, US banks neither have the size nor the historical background to fill the role of main banks within financial keiretsu. Equity ownership of Japanese banks in non-banks has only recently been restricted to 5 percent. Prior to the 5 percent rule, Japanese banks were entitled to acquire up to 10 percent of the outstanding stock of a single *kabushiki-kaisha*. In addition, intercorporate relationships have a long tradition in Japan. In the prewar era, large, partly monopolistic zaibatsu controlled many sectors of the Japanese economy. In the United States, intercorporate relationships have always been regarded with suspicion. Every attempt to form industrial groups failed as a result of neoclassical anti-trust regulations. Under these circumstances, financial keiretsu cannot develop around major US banks.

Unlike German holding companies, US holding companies have to pay income tax on dividends received from a subsidiary unless they hold at least 80 percent of the subsidiary's outstanding stock.[230] Under these conditions, holding companies lose some of their advantages over neoclassical capital markets. Especially in case of medium levels of industry maturity and investment plasticity, potential efficiency advantages of holding companies over unintermediated and intermediated capital markets are likely to be offset by tax disadvantages. As a result, the upper diagonal of Figure 1.9 (above) will move closer to the south-east corner.

With the exception of specially regulated holding companies, such as utility or bank holding companies, US holding companies are furthermore under constant risk of becoming the target of anti-trust regulators. Since it is much easier to break up holding companies than multidivisional organizations, CEOs often prefer to integrate new acquisitions as divisions of a multidivisional structure instead of managing them as subsidiaries within a holding structure. The 80 percent plus tax rule further facilitates the decision in favor of a multidivisional structure. As a result, the lower diagonal of Figure 1.9 will move closer to the north-west corner. The combined effect of US tax and anti-trust regulations is a smaller efficiency corridor for holding companies.

Statistical test

The same ordered probit model which has been employed to test the theory of organizational response to capital market inefficiencies under Germany's relational regulation will be used to test the theoretical predictions of organizational response to capital market inefficiencies under US neoclassical regulations. Applying the same principles as in the German model, an investment relation i is classified as $MODE_i = 0$ if coordinated by the US capital market, as $MODE_i = 1$ if coordinated within a holding company structure, and as $MODE_i = 2$ if coordinated within a multidivisional organization.

Statistical results

The empirical results for the United States are based on a random sample of n = 50 corporations out of all domestic nonfinancial corporations contained in the S&P 500, S&P MidCap 400 and S&P SmallCap 600 Index. Special holding companies (e.g. utility holding companies), if selected, were excluded from the sample and replaced by another randomly chosen corporation. Appendix C of this book lists the names of all corporations included in the sample. The necessary data were obtained through interviews and the analysis of annual reports, 10-K reports and other corporate publications.

Table 2.8 reports the statistical results of the ordered probit routine. The chi-squared statistic refutes the hypothesis that all slopes on the nonconstant regressors (investment plasticity, industry maturity) are zero with an error probability of less than 1 percent.

The coefficients of both independent variables have the predicted positive sign. The results of the ordered probit routine report a statistically highly significant ($\alpha < 0.01$) correlation between the two independent variables (investment plasticity and industry maturity) and the prevailing mode of capital allocation and corporate governance. The correlation between the two independent variables is low. The model correctly predicted thirty-two out of fifty cases.

Table 2.8 Statistical results for the United States
Ordered Probit Model, Max. Likelihood Estimates
Log - Likelihood = -40.85648; Restricted (slope = 0) Log-L = -48.66266;
Chi-squared (2) = 15.61236; Significance level = 0.4072099E- 03

Variable	Coefficient	Std. Error	t-ratio	Prob $|t| \geqslant x$	Mean	Std.Dev.
Constant	-1.8359	0.6460	-2.842	0.00449		
Investment plasticity	0.74613E-01	0.2648E-01	2.817	0.00484	6.8240	8.3201
Industry maturity	0.43360	0.1617	2.682	0.00733	3.300	1.4604
μ_1	0.39469	0.1521	2.528	0.01146		

Correlation between independent variables = -0.14405; sample size n = 50; number of correct predictions = 32

These statistical results support the theory of organizational response to capital market inefficiencies under neoclassical capital market regulation. Multidivisional organizations (holding companies) are an efficient response to capital market inefficiencies in case of high (medium) levels of industry maturity and investment plasticity.

CONCLUSION

German AGs and KGaAs, Japanese *kabushiki-kaisha* and US corporations operate out of different financial systems. German companies are handicapped by underdeveloped equity and corporate bond markets. This handicap would be eliminated if, first, more companies were granted access to Germany's capital market, and second, a larger percentage of investors decided to participate in capital market transactions. Enhanced competition within Germany's investment sector, especially through the entry of foreign investment banks into Germany's investment market and the introduction of neoclassical regulatory elements (e.g. stricter accounting, disclosure and auditing rules), might promote Germany's capital market development.

At its current stage, Japan's hybrid regulatory environment seems to combine the better of two worlds. The neoclassical elements of Japan's regulatory environment enhance Japan's competitiveness within immature industries, while the relational elements enhance governance efficiency and promote Japan's competitiveness within mature industries. The current initiative of Japan's Liberal Democratic Party (LDP) and some of its coalition partners to lift the general ban on holding companies seems to jeopardize Japan's regulatory equilibrium.

In the United States, anti-takeover-oriented regulations have led to inefficiencies within holding companies and multidivisional organizations. Without takeover threads from LBO associations, the management of holding companies and multidivisional organizations enjoys extensive discretionary freedoms. The highly fragmented ownership structure of US corporations does not provide enough governance incentives to effectively reduce these discretionary freedoms. Takeover-oriented capital market regulations could eliminate the prevailing inefficiencies.

SUMMARY

Unintermediated capital markets, fund-intermediated capital markets, bank-intermediated capital markets, holding companies, multidivisional organizations, leveraged buyout associations and financial keiretsu are alternative modes of capital allocation and corporate governance. If unintermediated capital markets were perfect, the prevailing organizational variety of capital allocation and corporate governance could not be explained in efficiency terms. If capital market imperfections prevail, however, alternative modes of capital allocation and corporate governance can be explained as a response to capital market inefficiencies.

In a world of organizational imperfections, organizational efficiency is not an absolute, but a relative attribute. An organizational mode of capital allocation and corporate governance can only be labeled "efficient" in comparison with other, consequently "inefficient" modes of capital allocation and corporate governance. In a multidimensional world, alternative organizational modes possess comparative advantages and disadvantages. Hence, relative organizational efficiency is not a general, but a situational attribute. An organizational mode which is efficient in one situation may be inefficient in another.

Based on these foundations, I have developed a theoretical framework which explains the prevailing variety of alternative organizational modes of capital allocation and corporate governance in terms of comparative situational efficiency. Within this theoretical framework, investment relations between investors (savers) and firms (defined as non-separable production and marketing units) represent the basic unit of analysis. Investment relation costs are the efficiency criterion. They consist of misallocation and governance costs. Misallocation costs represent the economic disadvantages

161

which result whenever scarce capital is not allocated to its (expected) highest-yield uses. Governance costs include all economic disadvantages which result from the potential conflict of interests between investors (savers) and corporate executives. The amount of investment relation costs (IRC_i) which are incurred during any given investment relation i depends on, first, the relevant characteristics of the underlying investment situation, and second, the organizational mode (OM_i) which is employed to coordinate the investment relation.

The relevant characteristics of the underlying investment situation are determined by, first, the regulatory environment (RE_i), and second, the relevant dimensions of the investment relation. Since the level of industry maturity (IM_i) and the degree of investment plasticity (IP_i) were identified as the relevant dimensions of an investment relation i, the developed theoretical model may be formalized as follows:

$$IRC_i = f(RE_i; IM_i; IP_i; OM_i) \text{ for all } i$$

Neoclassical and relational regulations have been identified as the extreme poles of a wide spectrum of potential regulatory environments. Neoclassical regulation is based on the theoretical ideal of perfect competition: all market participants are fully informed (i.e. information is costless) and take prices as given (i.e. they cannot manipulate prices). Under these ideal circumstances, the price mechanism will allocate scarce capital to its (expected) highest-yield uses. Real capital markets, however, differ from the neoclassical ideal. Consequently, neoclassical regulation tries to eliminate existing capital market imperfections. Extensive, well-specified and well-enforced accounting, auditing and disclosure rules will reduce the information asymmetries between corporate insiders and outsiders. Prohibition of insider trading is meant to attract a large number of capital market participants by eliminating the remaining information advantages of corporate insiders. Prohibition of market manipulation enhances the informational efficiency of market prices. Diversification requirements, anti-takeover laws and prohibition of universal banking all promote the neoclassical ideal of price-taking behavior by market participants.

While neoclassical regulation focuses on allocative efficiency, relational regulation concentrates on governance efficiency. From a relational perspective, neoclassical capital market imperfections are scrutinized with regard to their effect on corporate governance.

Information asymmetries, market manipulation, insider trading and universal banking are perceived as means to encourage ownership concentration and to promote corporate governance. Insider trading, for example, enables small shareholders to compensate large shareholders for their governance activities and nondiversification costs.

The level of industry maturity determines the type of knowledge which is necessary to allocate scarce capital to its highest-yield uses. Common and scattered knowledge are necessary to efficiently allocate scarce capital within immature industries. Common and insider knowledge are necessary to efficiently allocate scarce capital within mature industries.

The level of investment plasticity determines the governance problems which are associated with an investment relation. Investment relations which are characterized by low levels of investment plasticity do not cause major governance problems. Corporate executives either have small discretionary freedoms or can easily be monitored. Investment relations which are characterized by high levels of investment plasticity cause major governance problems. Corporate executives enjoy wide discretion and monitoring costs are substantial.

Unintermediated and intermediated capital markets, holding companies, multidivisional organizations, leveraged buyout associations and financial keiretsu are alternative modes of organizing investment relations. These alternative modes differ with respect to knowledge utilization, risk diversification and agency costs.

German AGs and KGaAs cannot economize on this organizational variety. While financial keiretsu and LBO associations are unlikely to evolve in Germany's regulatory environment, capital markets, holding companies and multidivisional organizations do not enjoy significant governance or allocation advantages over each other.

Germany's relational capital market regulations encourage ownership concentration. Almost three out of four listed corporations have a major shareholder who controls at least 50 percent of the voting rights. In case of ownership fragmentation, privileged universal banks act as delegated monitors via proxy voting and board representation. Under these circumstances, holding companies and multidivisional organizations do not provide superior governance structures for the coordination of investment relations which are characterized by high levels of investment plasticity.

Ownership concentration and the dominance of privileged universal banks result in underdeveloped equity and corporate bond markets. As a result of relational regulations, corporate outsiders will either refrain from capital market transactions at all or prefer long-term investment strategies. Under these circumstances, Germany's weak equity and corporate bond markets reflect substantial amounts of insider knowledge, but cannot aggregate and transmit sufficient amounts of scattered knowledge. Consequently, relational capital markets cannot allocate scarce capital within immature industries more efficiently than holding companies or multidivisional organizations.

Japan's hybrid regulatory environment combines relational and neoclassical elements. Although holding companies are prohibited and LBO associations are unlikely to emerge under Japanese regulations, Japan's *kabushiki-kaisha* are able to economize on the remaining organizational variety.

As a result of its neoclassical elements, Japan's capital market is able to aggregate and transmit large amounts of scattered knowledge in order to allocate scarce capital to high-yield uses within immature industries. Based on neoclassical accounting, disclosure and auditing rules, Japan's capital market provides efficient governance structures for investment relations which are characterized by low levels of investment plasticity. Investment relations whose degrees of industry maturity and investment plasticity exceed medium levels but do not reach high levels are efficiently organized within financial keiretsu. If investment plasticity and industry maturity reach high levels, Japan's capital market and financial keiretsu will be outperformed by multidivisional organizations.

US capital market regulations represent the prototype of neoclassical regulation. As a result, corporate ownership is highly fragmented. The price mechanism efficiently allocates scarce capital within immature industries. Strict accounting, disclosure and auditing regulations guarantee efficient market governance of investment relations whose degree of investment plasticity does not exceed medium levels.

Since financial keiretsu cannot emerge under US regulations, holding companies are the efficient mode of organizing investment relations which are characterized by medium levels of industry maturity and investment plasticity. However, the efficiency spectrum of US holding companies is highly limited because of neoclassical antitrust regulations and tax disadvantages. Many corporations prefer to integrate subsidiaries as divisions of a multidivisional structure as soon as the underlying degrees of industry maturity and investment plasticity have reached medium-to-high levels. Since the efficiency of holding companies and multidivisional organizations relies on the presence of LBO associations and the existence of an active market for corporate control, anti-takeover regulations impair organizational efficiency.

APPENDICES

APPENDIX A

German corporations included in the sample for the statistical test

AESCULAP Aktiengesellschaft
Allgemeine Gold- und Silberscheideanstalt Aktiengesellschaft
Audi Aktiengesellschaft
Bayerische Wasserkraftwerke Aktiengesellschaft
Bien-Haus Aktiengesellschaft
Dortmunder Actien-Brauerei Aktiengesellschaft
edding Aktiengesellschaft
ESCADA Aktiengesellschaft
Gold-Zack Werke Aktiengesellschaft
Friedrich Grohe Aktiengesellschaft
Hagen Batterie AG
Heilit & Woerner Bau-AG
Herlitz International Trading Aktiengesellschaft
Hofer Bierbrauerei Aktiengesellschaft Deininger-Kronenbräu
Karstadt Aktiengesellschaft
Krauss-Maffei Aktiengesellschaft
G. Kromschröder Aktiengesellschaft
KWS Kleinwanzlebener Saatzucht Aktiengesellschaft vorm.
    Rabbethge & Giesecke
Lindner Holding Kommanditgesellschaft auf Aktien
Löwenbräu Holding Aktiengesellschaft
Parkbrauerei Aktiengesellschaft Pirmasens-Zweibrücken
PESAG Aktiengesellschaft
PREUSSAG Aktiengesellschaft

Quante Aktiengesellschaft
Rathgeber Aktiengesellschaft
Sixt Aktiengesellschaft
Spinnerei und Weberei Momm Aktiengesellschaft
Thyssen Aktiengesellschaft vorm. August Thyssen-Hütte
TIPTEL Aktiengesellschaft
Triton-Belco Aktiengesellschaft
Wünsche Aktiengesellschaft

APPENDIX B

Japanese corporations included in the sample for the statistical test

Akebono Brake Industry Co. Ltd. (Akebono Brake Kogyo)
Asahi Glass Co. Ltd.
Canon Inc.
Citizen Watch Co. Ltd. (Citizen Tokei)
CSK Corp.
Dai Nippon Toryo Co. Ltd.
Daiichi Pharmaceutical Co. Ltd. (Daiichi Seiyaku)
Daimei Telecom Engineering Corp. (Daimei)
Denki Kagaku Kogyo Co. Ltd.
DYNIC Corp.
EBARA Corp.
Fukusuke Corp.
Furukawa Electric Co. Ltd. (Furukawa Denki Kogyo)
Furuno Electric Co. Ltd. (Furuno Denki)
Hitachi Powdered Metals Co. Ltd. (Hitachi Funmatsu Yakin)
Hochiki Corp.
Honda Motor Co. Ltd. (Honda Giken Kogyo)
Kagome Co. Ltd.
Kaneka Corp. (Kanegafuchi Kagaku Kogyo)
Kanto Special Steel Works Ltd. (Kantoku)
Kayaba Industry Co. Ltd. (Kayaba Kogyo)
LINTEC Corp.
Matsushita Communication Industrial Co. Ltd. (Matsushita Tsushin
    Kogyo)
Mitsubishi Corp. (Mitsubishi Shoji)
Mitsui High-tec Inc.

Mitsui Mining & Smelting Co. Ltd. (Mitsui Kinzoku Kogyo)
Mitsui Mining Co. Ltd. (Mitsui Kozan)
Mitsukoshi Ltd.
Nachi-Fujikoshi Corp. (Fujikoshi)
NAMCO Ltd.
NEC Corp. (Nippon Denki)
Neturen Co. Ltd. (Koshuha Netsuren)
Nippon Densetsu Kogyo Co. Ltd.
Nippon Express Co. Ltd. (Nippon Tsuun)
Nippon Steel Corp. (Shin Nippon Seitetsu)
Nishimatsu Construction Co. Ltd. (Nishimatsu Kensetsu)
Okabe Co. Ltd.
Olympus Optical Co. Ltd. (Olympus Kogaku Kogyo)
Osaka Sanso Kogyo Ltd.
Rinnai Corp.
Sanoyas Hishino Meisho Corp.
Sanyo Electric Co. Ltd. (San'yo Denki)
Sekisui House Ltd.
ShinMaywa Industries Ltd. (ShinMaywa Kogyo)
SMC Corp.
Tamura Electric Works Ltd. (Tamura Denki Seisakusho)
TEAC Corp.
Tomoku Co. Ltd.
Topre Corp.
Toyo Ink Mfg Co. Ltd. (Toyo Ink Seizo)

APPENDIX C

US corporations included in the sample for the statistical test

Advance Circuits Inc.
Amgen Inc.
Amtrol Inc.
Arrow Electronics Inc.
Ashland Oil Inc.
Borden Inc.
Bowne & Co. Inc.
Briggs & Stratton Corporation
Charming Shoppes Inc.
Circuit City Stores Inc.

Dole Food Company Inc.
Eli Lilly and Company
EMC Corporation
Flowers Industries Inc.
Franklin Quest Co.
Grow Group Inc.
Guilford Mills Inc.
Hershey Foods Corporation
Homestake Mining Company
Hubbel Incorporated
IMC Fertilizer Group Inc.
IMCO Recycling Inc.
Integrated Device Technology Inc.
Invacare Corporation
Jacobs Engineering Group Inc.
James River Corporation of Virginia
Johnston Industries Inc.
Lancaster Colony Corporation
Mark IV Industries Inc.
Michael Foods Inc.
Millipore Corporation
Morrison Restaurants Inc.
Morton International Inc.
Navistar International Corporation
Network Equipment Technologies Inc.
Oak Industries Inc.
OHM Corporation
Olin Corporation
Omnicom Group Inc.
Phillips-Van Heusen Corporation
Santa Fe Pacific Gold Corporation
The Score Board Inc.
Seitel Inc.
Southdown Inc.
Staples Inc.
StrataCom Inc.
United States Surgical Corporation
WD-40 Company
Westinghouse Electric Corporation
Whitman Corporation

NOTES

1 THEORETICAL FRAMEWORK

1 The following argument has been developed in analogy to Allen's (1993: 90–2) analysis of the true and perceived relationship between managerial actions and firm value.

2 Originally, Jensen and Meckling (1976: 308) defined agency costs as the sum of "(1) the monitoring expenditures by the principal, (2) the bonding expenditures by the agent, (3) the residual loss." Due to the existing literature on job market signaling and screening (e.g. Arrow 1973; Spence 1973, 1974; Stiglitz 1975a), the term "bonding expenditures" was not accepted, but replaced by the term "signaling costs." In addition, screening costs were added as a separate component.

3 Credible commitments enable potential investors to distinguish honest partners from mere charlatans. For the importance of credible commitments in supporting exchange relations see Williamson (1983).

4 The term "active investor" refers to a person "who actually monitors management, sits on boards, is sometimes involved in dismissing management, is often intimately involved in the strategic direction of the company, and on occasion even manages. That description fits Carl Icahn, Irwin Jacobs, and Kohlberg, Kravis, Roberts (KKR)" (Jensen 1989: 36).

5 Note here that proxy contests, although regarded by some as a substitute for takeovers (e.g. Gavin 1990), do not effectively replace takeovers as a means of disciplining management. The free-rider problem that inhibits small shareholders from incurring monitoring costs applies in spades to initiating a proxy contest. "The full costs are borne by the challengers in every case, yet they obtain reimbursement only if they prevail, and they obtain the gains (if any) from changes in management only in proportion to their equity interests" (Easterbrook and Fischel 1991: 78). The cost-benefit asymmetries make proxy fights an inefficient means of reducing the agency costs of delegated management (see also Gilson 1981).

6 The level of capital market liquidity is determined by the degree of market continuity and market depth (see Reilly 1985). Market continuity is measured by the price differences from one transaction to the

next. While market continuity describes a dynamic aspect, market depth refers to a static aspect. Market depth is measured by the number of market participants who are willing to trade at prices slightly above or below the current market price.

7   This extended definition is also employed by the World Bank (1989: 50).

8   The term "knowledge links" was introduced by Badaracco (1991) to describe a network of personal relationships among business executives which facilitates the transmission of tacit knowledge.

9   Only international competition from neoclassically regulated investment banks may prevent this erosion.

10 As Alchian and Woodward (1987: 123) indicate, the governance advantages of concentrated ownership rights may explain why gross returns are abnormally high in firms where insider trading is significant. Outsiders earn competitive returns and insiders are rewarded with superior returns.

11 See Dietl and Picot (1995: 30). A similar taxonomy has been introduced by Schmidt (1984: 342–6) who distinguishes between "event" and "model information." Both taxonomies are different from Manne's (1966: 47–57) concept of "first-" and "second-category information."

12 On the limitations of human information processing see for example Simon (1957).

13 The necessary conditions for perfect capital markets are described for example in Copeland and Weston (1988: 331), Franke and Hax (1994: 337), Schmidt and Terberger (1996: 88–95).

14 The investment preferences of non-owner managers depend upon their compensation plans. Corporate executives whose compensation plan is based on their corporation's market value possess similar investment preferences as corporate owners. Corporate executives who receive fixed salaries possess similar investment preferences as corporate creditors. Consequently, it can be assumed that executive compensation is less sensitive to changes in the residual income within bank-dominated systems than it is within market-dominated systems.

15 See Stiglitz and Weiss (1981, 1985, 1987a, 1987b). Note that early literature on credit rationing exists (e.g. Jaffee and Modigliani 1969). However, this literature only restated, not explained, the existence of credit rationing. Stiglitz and Weiss (1983) use the same arguments which explain credit rationing to explain why firms use termination rather than wage cuts to reduce their wage expenses.

16 Bester (1985) and Chan and Kanatas (1985) have developed formal models to discuss the economic role of collateral as an institutional device to obviate credit rationing.

17 A detailed description of the term "asset specificity" is presented among others by Lachmann (1956: 2–3), Klein *et al.* (1978: 298–302), Williamson (1979: 238–45), Alchian (1984: 36–8) and Joskow (1988: 103–15). According to Williamson (1985: 52) the awareness of the condition described as asset specificity can be traced back to Marshall (1948: 453–4) who expresses conditions of asset specificity

in connection with the term "composite-quasi-rent." "A quasi-rent is the excess above the return necessary to maintain a resource's current service flow. . . . Composite quasi-rent is that portion of the quasi-rent of resources that depends on continued association with some other specific, currently associated resources."

18 For a complete classification and detailed description of bond covenants see Smith and Warner (1979) or Copeland and Weston (1988: 512).

19 The theory of credit rationing is compatible with the fact that bonds which are denominated in weak currencies carry an interest rate premium. The theory of credit rationing is also compatible with the fact that bond prices (and the resulting interest rates) in the secondary market may reveal the default risk of the issuer.

20 The theory of signaling has been introduced by Spence (1973, 1974).

21 To be effective, reputation requires a continuous flow of profits, otherwise there would be no incentive to build and maintain a reputation (see Greenwald and Stiglitz 1991: 19–20).

22 The empirical evidence is summarized in Smith (1986). Asquith and Mullins (1986), for example, found that on average stock prices decreased by 2.7 percent in response to the announcement of a seasoned equity issue.

23 These studies are based on the transactions reported by corporate insiders to the Securities and Exchange Commission in the United States. Under US law, corporate insiders, defined as all officers, directors and owners of 10 percent or more of any class of equity, must report their stock transactions to the Securities and Exchange Commission.

24 Chart analysts cannot beat the market as long as current prices fully reflect all historical price information.

25 For general discussion of voice and exit as alternative reactions of dissatisfied principals, see Hirschman (1970).

26 If share prices signal which corporations are undervalued, *ex post* competition among bidders is limited. "This is so because generally one raider will be first to discover what changes should be made in a corporation, and since other raiders do not have this knowledge, they will not be able to compete effectively with the informed raider" (Grossman and Hart 1980: 58).

27 For a more complete overview of potential shareholder exploitation by fund advisors/administrators see for example Wharton School (1962: 27–36), US Securities and Exchange Commission (1963: 144, 148), (1966: 16–17).

28 The entire downside risk is still borne by shareholders, who have their capital at stake.

29 For a more detailed analysis of entry conditions in the fund industry see Baumol *et al.* (1990: 122–5)

30 The importance of transformation services, especially liquidity creation, is emphasized by Niehans (1978: 166–84).

31 The term "consolidation" was introduced by Fisher (1906: 291–5).

32 The economic value of the liquidity transformation process is expressed by Tobin's (1965: 7–11) theory of liquidity preference. A

modern explanation of liquidity preference is provided by Gorton and Pennacchi (1990) who interpret liquidity preference as a rational response of uninformed investors. Uninformed investors who are aware of their information disadvantage will prefer liquid, i.e. information-insensitive, securities because ownership of illiquid, i.e. information-sensitive, securities would expose them to exploitation by informed investors.

33 Other concepts of liquidity such as the one introduced by Patinkin do not allow the same precision in distinguishing risk from liquidity. According to Patinkin (1965: 118) liquidity represents "the absence of uncertainty with respect to the future real value of an asset."

34 The entire risk associated with an initial public offering is composed of a waiting risk, a pricing risk and a marketing risk (see Bloch 1986: 152–7). The waiting risk refers to unexpected price changes that occur during the time period between the pricing decision and legal effectiveness of the offering. Pricing risk includes improper pricing in a stable market and proper pricing overwhelmed by an unstable market. Offering the issue to the wrong people or at the wrong time are the major marketing errors.

35 Self-selection describes the process by which an agent who is guided by self-interest and whose characteristics are unknown to the principal automatically chooses the efficient contract out of a variety of contracts offered by the principal and thereby reveals his or her unknown characteristics.

36 See also Kraus and Stoll (1972: 573) who conclude that "blocks are sold, not bought."

37 For further insight into block trading see Burdett and O'Hara (1987).

38 Note that the underpricing equilibrium may be interpreted as the counterpart of equity markets to credit rationing in debt markets. However, equity rationing affects the size of each equity offering, whereas credit rationing limits the number of debt contracts.

39 See for example D'Artista (1994: 82) and the references cited therein.

40 See for example Fischer et al. (1984).

41 For a more extensive discussion of the risk effects of universal banking see Benston (1990).

42 For further comparisons see Daems (1978: 34–5).

43 For a description of the shareholder value concept see Rappaport (1986).

44 See for example Heflebower (1960), Alchian (1969), Williamson and Bhargava (1972).

45 For an extensive analysis of the growth and diversification effects associated with the introduction of the multidivisional structure see Chandler (1962) and Williamson (1981).

46 Jensen (1989: 38) estimates the pay-to-performance sensitivity of a multidivisional organization's CEO at $3.25 per $1,000 and that of a LBO unit's leading manager at $64 per $1,000.

47 LBOs, on the other hand, protect themselves against sharp increases in interest rates by purchasing caps or using swaps. These protective

measures are commonly required by lending banks as a condition for providing loans (see Jensen 1989: 4).

48 For an investigation into the sources of value in leveraged buyouts see Kaplan (1988), Jensen (1991), Long and Ravenscraft (1991).

49 City banks typically lend on a three-month basis. Top-rated borrowers are charged the short-term prime rate which lies about one-half of a percentage point above the official discount rate (see Bronte 1982: 16–17).

50 For the informational role of debt in general see Harris and Raviv (1990).

51 Note here that each keiretsu also includes a casualty insurance company. Analogous to life insurance companies, casualty insurance companies receive most of the keiretsu's casualty insurance business in return for channeling their debt and equity investments primarily to keiretsu members. Compared to the financial institutions which constitute the keiretsu's financial core, however, casualty insurance companies are less important because of their smaller size and so are omitted here.

52 Focusing on long-term lending disqualifies trust banks and insurance companies as an efficient monitor of fellow keiretsu firms. Trading companies and city banks, both of whom are primarily engaged in short-term lending, have access to more up-to-date inside information and are able to install more effective disciplinary measures than trust banks and life insurance companies. The privilege of offering payment services to their customers gives city banks another information advantage compared to trust banks and life insurance companies, who have no immediate access to ongoing deposit information. For the economic value of deposit information see Fama (1985).

53 Note here that each keiretsu network usually consists of no more than one firm per industry. Thus profits among keiretsu firms are highly uncorrelated. For further discussion of the stabilization of corporate performance within keiretsu networks see Nakatani (1984: 242–5).

54 Security ownership by investment companies and investment trusts is usually limited to 5 or 10 percent of a corporation's outstanding stocks and bonds.

55 Consider, for example, an assembly line which consists of single-purpose machines or a license to use a certain patent. In case of the assembly line, technological rigidities guarantee that the respective assets are used in the desired way, wheras legal restraints restict the usage of patent licenses.

56 Neoclassical regulation forces investors who hold more than a certain percentage (usually 5 percent) of a corporation's outstanding shares to disclose all their trades in this corporation's securities.

57 As insiders, these investors are always under suspicion of trading on the basis of private yet undisclosed inside information. This suspicion practically precludes them from trading prior to public announcements, such as earnings reports or public offerings.

58 Under neoclassical regulation, major investors may be held liable for the actions of the corporation (see e.g. Meyer 1934: 127).

59 Under neoclassical regulation, financial intermediaries are usually not allowed to invest more than a certain percentage (3–5 percent) of their proceeds in securities of a single corporation, or to acquire more than a certain percentage (5–10 percent) of a single corporation's outstanding shares.

2 EMPIRICAL EVIDENCE

1   AktG §§ 278–90.
2   AktG §§ 1–277.
3   AktG § 60.
4   AktG § 271.
5   AktG § 131.
6   AktG § 134.
7   AktG §134 (1).
8   AktG § 12 (2).
9   AktG § 139 (1).
10 AktG §§ 118–47.
11 AktG § 120.
12 AktG § 101.
13 AktG §§ 119 (4), 142.
14 AktG § 174.
15 AktG § 179 (2).
16 AktG §§ 182 (1), 193 (1), 202 (2), 207 (2).
17 AktG §§ 222 (1), 229 (3), 237 (2).
18 AktG § 262 (2).
19 AktG § 319 (2).
20 AktG §§ 340 (c) (2), 353 (3).
21 AktG § 362 et seq.
22 AktG §§ 76–94.
23 AktG §§ 95–116.
24 Partnerships which do not issue shares are excluded from the regulations even if they employ more than 500 people.
25 It does not apply to general, limited and dormant partnerships. It does apply, however, to limited partnerships whose general partner is a company with limited liability.
26 HGB § 252 (1) no. 4.
27 HGB § 253 (2), (3).
28 HGB § 252 (1) no. 4.
29 AktG § 150.
30 *Einkommenssteuergesetz* or EStG ("Tax Code") § 5 (1).
31 A GmbH (*Gesellschaft mit beschränkter Haftung* or limited liability company) is a private limited corporation. GmbHs do not issue share certificates unless required under company statutes. Even if share certificates have been issued, they are not recognized as legal evidence of ownership under German law. Transfer of share certificates requires a formal contract which is attested by a notary (*Gesetz betreffend die Gesellschaften mit beschränkter Haftung*—GmbHG § 15 (3)). Moreover,

company statutes may provide that any transfer of GmbH certificates must be approved by the company. Consequently, GmbH shares cannot be traded on stock exchanges. As a result, GmbHs are much more dependent on bank intermediation than AGs or KGaAs. At year-end 1993, there were 543,444 GmbHs and 2,934 (listed and non-listed) AGs and KGaAs registered in Germany. The 543,444 GmbHs represented a nominal capital of DM235.3 billion, while the 2,934 AGs and KGaAs represented a nominal capital of DM147.3 billion. (Statistisches Jahrbuch für die Bundesrepublik Deutschland, 1995: 132).

32 *Publizitätsgesetz* or PublG ("Disclosure Act"); HGB §§ 264–335.
33 HGB §§ 242 (3); 264 (1).
34 HGB §§ 316–24; PublG § 6.
35 HGB §§ 325, 328; PublG § 9.
36 HGB §§ 265, 266, 268, 275, 277, 278, 281, 282; PublG § 5 (1).
37 HGB § 284 (2).
38 HGB § 285 no. 5.
39 HGB § 285 no. 9 (a), (b).
40 HGB § 285 no. 9 (c).
41 HGB § 285 no. 4.
42 AktG § 160 (1) no. 2.
43 HGB § 285 no. 11.
44 HGB § 285 no. 7.
45 HGB § 289.
46 HGB § 290.
47 *Börsengesetz* or BG ("Security Exchange Act") § 44b (1).
48 *Börsenzulassungsverordnung* or BörsZulV ("Enforcement Order Regarding the Security Exchange Act") § 54 (1).
49 BörsZulV § 53.
50 BG § 44a (1); *Wertpapierhandelsgesetz* or WpHG ("Securities Trade Law") § 15 (1).
51 WpHG § 21 (1).
52 WpHG §§ 13, 14, 38.
53 WpHG § 32 (2).
54 Germany's first hostile takeover occurred when Bopp & Reuther AG was acquired by Industrie-Werke Karlsruhe Augsburg AG.
55 AG § 84 (1) and (3).
56 Such statutes which must be approved by a three-quarters majority have been passed, among others, by BASF AG (DM80 million of nominal equity), Bayer AG (5 percent), Continental AG (5 percent), Linde AG (10 percent), Mannesmann AG (5 percent), Schering AG (DM12 million of nominal equity) and Volkswagen AG (20 percent).
57 AG §§ 340 (c) (2); 361 (1).
58 AG § 340 (a), (b).
59 *Gesetz über Kapitalanlagegesellschaften* or KAGG ("Investment Company Act") § 8 (a) (1).
60 *Versicherungsaufsichtsgesetz or* VAG ("Insurance Supervisory Law") § 54 (a) (5).
61 For example, Germany's largest corporation (if measured in terms of market capitalization), Allianz Aktiengesellschaft Holding, an insur-

ance holding and reinsurance company, owns, among many other direct and indirect holdings, 25 percent of Münchener Rück-versicherungs-Gesellschaft AG, the world's largest reinsurance company, 22 percent of Dresdner Bank AG, Germany's second largest bank, 22 percent of Bayerische Hypotheken- und Wechsel-Bank AG, Germany's sixth largest bank, and 37 percent of Beiersdorf AG, a large chemical company.

62 *Gesetz über das Kreditwesen or KWG* ("Banking Act") § 1.

63 AktG § 135. For many years German banks were virtually automatically entitled to an indefinite time for exercising proxy voting rights for all shares deposited with them without requiring any instructions from actual shareholders. For an overview of the history of the *Vollmachtsstimmrecht* see Wenger (1992: 76–81).

64 AktG § 135 (2).

65 AktG § 128 (2).

66 AktG § 128 (2).

67 AktG § 135 (5).

68 AktG § 135 (1).

69 KWG § 10. In accordance with the Second Banking Directive of the European Community, the credit risk equivalents of swaps, futures and options have to be included in the calculation.

70 For an overview of the German deposit insurance mechanism and the capital requirements of German banks see Rudolph (1993).

71 The adjustment is necessary because intercorporate shareholdings inflate total market capitalization. For more details see Dewatripont and Tirole (1994: 74–7).

72 The stock exchanges are located in Frankfurt, Düsseldorf, Munich, Hamburg, Stuttgart, Berlin, Hanover and Bremen.

73 Averages are weighted averages with weights given by nominal capital of each corporation.

74 Eighteen were subsidiaries of foreign firms, eleven were subsidiaries of domestic firms, nine had a family or private foundation as majority shareholder and six were government-owned.

75 Unweighted averaged.

76 Own calculations based on Böhm (1992: 257–62, Table 42).

77 See Deutsche Bundesbank (1990).

78 See Deutsche Bundesbank (1990).

79 The ordered probit model was developed by Zavoina and McKelvey (1975).

80 The common alternative to the ordered probit model, the ordered logit model, assumes that the ε_i have a standard logistic instead of a standard normal distribution. Since the difference between both distributions is small (with exception of the tails), the results should not be sensitive to the choice between both models, unless there is a large number of observation in the tails (see e.g. Maddala 1983).

81 Japanese Commercial Code (CC), Articles 165–456.

82 CC Article 222 (1).

83 CC Article 242.

84 CC Article 241 (1).

85 CC Article 200 (1).
86 CC Article 234 (1).
87 CC Article 239 (1).
88 CC Articles 245 (1); 280–2 (2); 342 (1); 343; 375 (1); 405.
89 CC Article 254 (1).
90 CC Article 255.
91 CC Article 256 (1) and (2).
92 CC Articles 257 (1), (3); 343.
93 CC Article 260 (1).
94 CC Article 260 (2).
95 CC Article 260.2 (1).
96 CC Article 261 (1).
97 CC Article 269.
98 CC Article 274.
99 CC Article 276.
100 CC Article 273 (1) and (2).
101 CC Articles 280; 254 (1); 257 (1), (2); 343; 279 (1).
102 CC Article 319.
103 CC Article 320 (1).
104 CC Article 320 (3).
105 CC Article 321 (1).
106 CC Articles 309-2 (1); 324; 343.
107 CC Articles 324; 329 (1); 330 (1); 333; 343.
108 CC Articles 319; 324; 343.
109 CC Article 327 (1).
110 CC Article 326.
111 CC Article 281 (1).
112 CC Article 281(2).
113 Law for Special Exceptions to Commercial Code Concerning Audit, etc., of *Kabushiki-kaisha*, Article 2.
114 CC Article 283 (2).
115 CC Article 283 (1).
116 CC Article 285-2.
117 CC Article 285-6.
118 CC Article 34.
119 CC Article 288-2.
120 CC Article 288.
121 ARA Article 35-3.
122 ARA Article 45 (1) no. 9.
123 ARA Article 45 (2).
124 ARA Article 45 (1) no. 4.
125 ARA Article 45 (1) no. 7.
126 ARA Article 3.
127 ARA Article 47 no. 10.
128 ARA Article 47 no. 11
129 Financial Accounting Standards for Business Enterprises, Section III, 3.
130 Law for Special Exceptions to Commercial Code Concerning Audit, etc., of *Kabushiki-kaisha*, Article 16 (2).
131 SEL Article 4.

132 SEL Article 24 (1); 24-5 (1), (2).
133 SEL Article 25 (1).
134 Ministerial Ordinance Concerning Notification, etc., of Offering or Secondary Distribution of Securities, Article 17.
135 SEL Article 173-2.
136 FSR Article 42.
137 FSR Article 43.
138 FSR Articles 44; 56.
139 FSR Article 58.
140 FSR Article 68-2.
141 FSR Article 71.
142 Ministerial Ordinance Concerning Notification, etc. of offering or Secondary Distribution of Securities Article 19 (1).
143 SEL Articles 166; 167.
144 SEL Articles 200 (6); 197 (8).
145 SEL Article 163.
146 SEL Article 27-23 (1).
147 SEL Article 27-25 (2).
148 SEL Articles 157 (1)–(3); 158; 159-1; 159-2; 168.
149 Securities and Exchange Law Enforcement Order Articles 20–6.
150 SEL Article 133.
151 SEL Articles 27-2; 27-3; 5; 7–11.
152 SEL Article 27-4 (2).
153 SEL Article 27-4 (2).
154 Securities and Exchange Law Enforcement Order, Article 13 nos 1, 3, 4.
155 Securities and Exchange Law Enforcement Order, Article 13 no. 5.
156 Securities and Exchange Law Enforcement Order, Article 13 no. 8.
157 Note that there are no investment companies in Japan.
158 Securities Investment Trust Law, Article 17 (3) in combination with Ministry of Finance Ordinance no. 119 (for investment trusts) and Law Concerning Prohibition of Private Monopoly and Maintenance of Fair Trade, Article 11 (1) (for insurance companies).
159 Enforcement Order of the Insurance Business Law, Article 19 (1).
160 Law Concerning Prohibition of Private Monopoly and Maintenance of Fair Trade, Article 11 (1).
161 Securities and Exchange Law, Articles 2 (8) and 65 (1).
162 Banking Law, Article 7.
163 Law Concerning Prohibition of Private Monopoly and Maintenance of Fair Trade, Article 9.
164 Prowse (1990) reports a strong correlation between the percentage of outstanding debt and the percentage of outstanding equity held in the same firm by the largest debtholders. Although Prowse's study is based on empirical data from 1980–4, a period during which banks were allowed to hold up to 10 percent of a single firm's outstanding equity (compared to the current 5 percent rule), it supports the hypothesis that banks try to reduce the default risk of their loans to non-banks by acquiring non-default decision rights.
165 See Hoshi *et al.* (1989).
166 See Prowse (1992) who finds that the efficiency of corporate

governance within Japanese non-keiretsu firms relies exclusively on ownership concentration, whereas the efficiency of corporate governance within keiretsu firms is not significantly related to ownership concentration. Prowse cites additional governance mechanisms, such as long-term commercial trading relationships among keiretsu members, as a reason for these differences.

167 RMBCA § 6.22.
168 *Gordon v. Elliman*, 306 N.Y. 456 (N.Y. 1954).
169 RMBCA §§ 8.03(d) and 8.08.
170 RMBCA § 10.03.
171 RMBCA § 11.01(a).
172 RMBCA § 11.02(a).
173 RMBCA § 14.02(b)(2) and (e).
174 RMBCA § 12.02.
175 RMBCA § 8.08.
176 RMBCA § 16.02.
177 RMBCA § 7.40–7.47.
178 RMBCA §§ 7.01; 7.02.
179 RMBCA § 7.22(a).
180 RMBCA § 7.25(c).
181 RMBCA § 6.40(a).
182 RMBCA § 6.21(b).
183 RMBCA § 6.21(a).
184 RMBCA § 6.31(c).
185 RMBCA § 8.40(a).
186 See *Tillis v. United Parts Inc.* (Fla App) 395 So 2d 518 (1981).
187 RMBCA § 8.06.
188 See *Kuehn v. Kuehn* (Colo App) 642 P2d 524 (1982).
189 See statement no. 115 of the Financial Accounting Standards Board (FASB), "Accounting for certain investments in debt and equity securities."
190 See AICPA Statement of Position no. 81–1, "Accounting for performance of construction-type and certain production-type contracts."
191 See Opinion no. 18 of the Accounting Principles Board (APB), "The equity method of accounting for investments in common stock."
192 See Accounting Research Bulletin no. 43, Chapter 4, of the Accounting Procedures Committee, "Inventory pricing," and the FASB's expansion draft of November 1993, "Accounting for the impairment of long-lived assets."
193 See Accounting Research Bulletin no. 43, Chapter 9, of the Accounting Procedures Committee, "Depreciation."
194 See Statement no. 109 of the FASB, "Accounting for income taxes."
195 See Opinion no. 15 of the APB, "Earnings per share."
196 See Accounting Research Bulletin no. 43, Chapter 7, of the Accounting Procedures Committee, "Capital accounts."
197 See Statement no. 115 of the FASB, "Accounting for certain investments in debt and equity securities."
198 See Statement no. 52 (13, 20) of the FASB, "Foreign currency translation."

199 See Statement no. 14 of the FASB, "Financial reporting for segments of a business enterprise."

200 See Statement no. 30 of the FASB, "Disclosure of information about major customers."

201 See Statement no. 89 of the FASB, "Financial reporting and changing prices."

202 15 U.S.C.A. § 78(m).

203 17 C.F.R. § 240.14(a)(3).

204 17 C.F.R. § 240.10(b)(5).

205 15 U.S.C.A. § 78p(a).

206 15 U.S.C.A. § 78p(b).

207 15 U.S.C.A. §§ 78i, 78j.

208 Securities Exchange Act of 1934 § 14(e), 15 U.S.C.A. § 78n(e).

209 Securities Exchange Act of 1934 § 13(d)(1), 15 U.S.C.A. § 78m(d)(1).

210 Securities Exchange Act of 1934 § 14(d)(5), 15 U.S.C.A. § 78n(d)(5).

211 Securities Exchange Act of 1934 § 14(d)(6), 15 U.S.C.A. § 78n(d)(6).

212 Securities Exchange Act of 1934 § 14 d)(7), 15 U.S.C.A. § 78n(d)(7).

213 Securities Exchange Act of 1934 § 13(d)–(e), 15 U.S.C.A. § 78m(d)–(e).

214 See for example the statement of the Supreme Court in *Edgar v. MITE Corp.*, 457 U.S. 624, 643–6 (1982).

215 See Bureau of National Affairs (1990).

216 For an overview of state anti-takeover laws see McGurn *et al.* (1989).

217 Investment Company Act of 1940 § 5(b)(1), 15 U.S.C.A. § 80a-5(b)(1).

218 Investment Company Act of 1940 § 2(a)(3), 15 U.S.C.A. § 80a-2(a)(2).

219 Investment Company Act of 1940 § 17(a)(1)–(2), 15 U.S.C.A. § 80a-17(a)(1)–(2).

220 Internal Revenue Code § 851(b)(4).

221 New York Insurance Law 140(a)(6) and (8), 1405(a)(6)(I), 1705(a)(1)–(2).

222 ERISA § 407(a)(2), U.S.C.A. § 1107(a)(2)..

223 ERISA § 404(a)(1)(B), 29 U.S.C.A. § 1104(a)(1)(B).

224 McFadden Act, Ch. 191, 44 Stat. 1224.

225 12 U.S.C.A. §§ 24, 78, 377, 378(a), and 335 and 221.

226 C.F.R. 9.18(b)(9)(ii); Interval Revenue Code 584(a)(2)-(b).

227 Bank Holding Company Act of 1956 § 3(d), 12 U.S.C.A. § 1843(d).

228 Bank Holding Company Act of 1956 § 4(c)(6)–(7), 12 U.S.C.A. § 1843(c)(6)–(7).

229 Grundfest (1990) and Roe (1990, 1994) have developed interesting political theories of ownership fragmentation in the United States. These theories attempt to explain the prevailing level of ownership fragmentation as a result of political processes which have consistently shifted power from corporate owners to corporate managers.

230 Internal Revenue Code Section 1504(a).

BIBLIOGRAPHY

Akerlof, G.A. (1970) "The Markets for 'lemons': qualitative uncertainty and the market mechanism," *Quarterly Journal of Economics*, 84, 3: 488–500.

Alchian, A. A. (1969) "Corporate management and property rights," in H. G. Manne (ed.) *Economic Policy and Regulation of Corporate Securities*, Washington, DC: American Enterprise Institute for Public Policy Research, 337–60.

——(1984) "Specificity, specialization and coalitions," *Zeitschrift für die gesamte Staatswissenschaft*, 140, 1: 34–49.

Alchian, A. A. and Woodward, S. (1987) "Reflections on the theory of the firm," *Journal of Institutional and Theoretical Economics*, 143, 1: 110–36.

Allen, F. A. (1993) "Stock markets and resource allocation," in C. Mayer and X. Vives (eds) *Capital Markets and Financial Intermediation*, Cambridge: Cambridge University Press, 81–108.

Ando, A. and Auerbach, A. J. (1988) "The cost of capital in the United States and Japan: a comparison," *Journal of the Japanese and International Economies*, 2, 2: 134–58.

Arrow, K. J. (1973) "Higher education as a filter," *Journal of Public Economics*, 2, 3: 193–216.

Arrow, K. J. and Hahn, F. H. (1971) *General Competitive Analysis*, San Francisco: Holden-Day.

Asquith, P. and Mullins, D. W. (1986) "Equity issues and offering dilution," *Journal of Financial Economics*, 15, 1–2: 61–89.

Badaracco, J. L. Jr (1991) *The Knowledge Link: How Firms Compete Through Strategic Alliances*, Boston, MA: Harvard University Press.

Baum, H. and Schaede, U. (1994) "Institutional investors and corporate governance in Japanese perspective," in T. Baums, R. M. Buxbaum and K. J. Hopt (eds) *Institutional Investors and Corporate Governance*, Berlin: deGruyter, 609–64.

Baumol, W. J., Panzar. J. C. and Willig, R. D. (1988) *Contestable Markets and the Theory of Industry Structure*, San Diego: Harbour Brace Jovanovich.

182

Baumol, W. J., Goldfeld, S. M., Gordon, L. A. and Koehn, M. F. (1990) *The Economics of Mutual Funds Markets: Competition versus Regulation*, Boston: Kluwer.

Beatty, R. P. and Ritter, J. R. (1986) "Investment banking, reputation and the underpricing of initial public offerings," *Journal of Financial Economics*, 15, 1–2: 213–32.

Benston, G. J. (1990) *The Separation of Commercial and Investment Banking: The Glass-Steagall Act Revisited and Reconsidered*, London: Macmillan.

Berlin, M. and Mester, L. J. (1992) "Debt covenants and renegotiation," *Journal of Financial Intermediation*, 2,2: 95–133.

Bester, H. (1985) "Screening versus rationing in credit markets with imperfect information," *American Economic Review*, 75, 4: 850–5.

Bhide, A. (1993) "The hidden costs of stock market liquidity," *Journal of Financial Economics*, 34, 1: 31–51.

Bloch, E. (1986) *Inside Investment Banking*, Homewood: Dow Jones-Irwin.

Böhm, J. (1992) *Der Einfluß der Banken auf Großunternehmen*, Hamburg: S + W Steuer- und Wirtschaftsverlag.

Bronte, S. (1982) *Japanese Finance: Markets and Institutions*, London: Euromoney Publications.

Burdett, K. and O'Hara, M. (1987) "Building blocks: an introduction to block 'trading'," *Journal of Banking and Finance*, 11, 2: 193–212.

Bureau of National Affairs (1990) "Forty-two states currently have anti-takeover laws, ABA Group told," *Securities Law Reporter*, 22, 17 August, 1216.

Carey, M., Prowse, S., Rea, J. and Udell, G. (1993) "The economics of private placements: a new look," *Financial Markets, Institutions and Instruments*, 2, 3: 1–66.

Chan, Y. S. and Kanatas, G. (1985) "Asymmetric valuations and the role of collateral in loan agreements," *Journal of Money, Credit and Banking*, 17, 1: 84–95.

Chandler, A. D. (1962) *Strategy and Structure*, Cambridge, MA: MIT Press.

Chemmanur, T. J. and Fulghieri, P. (1994) "Investment bank reputation, information production and financial intermediation," *Journal of Finance*, 49, 1: 57–79.

Copeland, T. E. and Weston, J. F. (1988) *Financial Theory and Corporate Policy*, 3rd ed., Reading: Addison-Wesley.

D'Artista, J. W. (1994) *The Evolution of US Finance, Volume II: Restructuring Institutions and Markets*, Armonk: M. E. Sharpe.

Daems, H. (1978) *The Holding Company and Corporate Control*, Leiden: Martinus Nijhoff.

Debreu, G. (1959) *Theory of Value*, New Haven, CT: Cowles Foundation.

Demsetz, H. and Lehn, K. (1985) "The structure of corporate ownership: causes and consequences," *Journal of Political Economy*, 93, 6: 1155–77.

Deutsche Bundesbank (1990) *Zahlenübersichten und methodische Erläuterungen zur gesamtwirtschaftlichen Finanzierungsrechnung der Deutschen Bundesbank 1960–89 sowie Ergänzungslieferung für das Jahr 1990* (Sonderdrucke der Deutschen Bundesbank Nr.4).

Dewatripont, M. and Tirole, J. (1994) *The Prudential Regulation of Banks*, Cambridge, MA: MIT Press.

Diamond, D. W. (1984) "Financial intermediation and delegated monitoring," *Review of Economic Studies*, 51, 3: 393–414.

Dietl, H. and Picot, A. (1995) "Information (de)regulation of capital markets from the viewpoint of new institutional economics," *Hitotsubashi Journal of Commerce and Management*, 30, 1: 29–46.

Dodwell Marketing Consultants (1994) *Industrial Groupings in Japan: The Anatomy of the Keiretsu*, Tokyo: Dodwell Marketing Consultants.

Drukarczyk, J. (1993) *Theorie und Politik der Finanzierung*, 2nd ed., Munich: Vahlen.

Easterbrook, F. H. and Fischel, D. R. (1991) *The Economic Structure of Corporate Law*, Cambridge, MA: Harvard University Press.

Fama, E. F. (1970) "Efficient capital markets: a review of theory and empirical work," *Journal of Finance*, 25, 2: 383–417.

——(1985) "What's different about banks?," *Journal of Monetary Economics*, 15, 1: 29–36.

Finnerty, J. E. (1976) "Insiders and market efficiency," *Journal of Finance*, 31, 4: 1141–8.

Fischer, T. G., Gram, W. H., Kaufman, G. G. and Mote, L. R. (1984) "The securities activities of commercial banks: a legal and economic analysis," *Tennessee Law Review*, 51, 3: 467–518.

Fisher, I. (1906) *The Nature of Capital and Income*, New York: Macmillan.

Franke, G. and Hax, H. (1994) *Finanzwirtschaft des Unternehmens und Kapitalmarkt*, 3rd ed., Berlin: Springer.

Friend, I. and Tokutsu, I. (1987) "The cost of capital to corporations in Japan and the USA," *Journal of Banking and Finance*, 11, 2: 313–27.

Friend, I., Blume, M. and Crockett, J. (1970) *Mutual Funds and Other Institutional Investors: A New Perspective*, New York: McGraw-Hill.

Gale, I. L. and Stiglitz, J. E. (1989) "The informational content of initial public offerings," *Journal of Finance*, 44, 2: 469–77.

Gavin, J. J. (1990) "Proxy contests emerge: supplant tender offers in seeking corporate change," *New York Law Journal*, 9 October: 7.

Gilson, R. J. (1981) "A structural approach to corporations: the case against defensive tactics in tender offers," *Stanford Law Review*, 33, 5: 819–91.

Gorton, G. and Pennacchi, G. (1990) "Financial intermediaries and liquidity creation," *Journal of Finance*, 45, 1: 49–71.

Gorton, G. and Schmid, F. A. (1994) "Universal banking and the performance of German firms," Working Paper, Wharton School.

Greenwald, B. C. and Stiglitz, J. E. (1991) "Information, finance and markets: the architecture of allocative mechanisms," NBER Working Paper no. 3652.

Grossman, S. J. and Hart, O. E. (1980) "Takeover bids, the free-rider problem and the theory of the corporation," *Bell Journal of Economics*, 11, 1: 42–64.

BIBLIOGRAPHY

Grossman, S. J. and Stiglitz, J. E. (1976) "Information and competitive price systems," *American Economic Review*, Papers and Proceedings, 66, 2: 246–53.

——(1980) "On the impossibility of informationally efficient markets," *American Economic Review*, 70, 3: 393–408.

Grundfest, J. A. (1990) "Subordination of American capital," *Journal of Financial Economics*, 27, 1: 89–114.

Harris, M. and Raviv, A. (1990) "The informational role of debt," *Journal of Finance*, 45, 2: 321–49.

Hayek, F. A. (1945) "The use of knowledge in society," *American Economic Review*, 35, 4: 519–30.

Heflebower, R. B. (1960) "Observation on decentralization in large enterprises," *Journal of Industrial Economics*, 9, 1: 7–22.

Henderson, D. F. (1991) "Security markets in the United States and Japan: distinctive aspects molded by cultural, social, economic and political differences," *Hastings International and Comparative Law Review*, 14, 2: 263–301.

Hirschman, A. O. (1970) *Exit, Voice and Loyalty*, Cambridge: Harvard University Press.

Horiuchi, A. (1989) "Informational properties of the Japanese financial system," *Japan and the World Economy*, 1, 3: 255–78.

Hoshi, T., Kashyap, A. and Scharfstein, D. (1989) "Bank monitoring and investment: evidence from the changing structure of Japanese corporate banking relationships," NBER Working Paper no. 3079.

Jaffe, J. F. (1974) "Special information and insider trading," *Journal of Business*, 47, 3: 410–28.

Jaffee, D. and Modigliani, F. (1969) "A theory and test of credit rationing," *American Economic Review*, 59, 5: 850–72.

Japan Securities Research Institute (1994) *Securities Market in Japan 1994*, Tokyo: Tokyo Shoken Kaikan.

Jensen, M. C. (1986) "Agency costs of free cash flow, corporate finance and takeovers," *American Economic Review*, 76, 2: 323–9.

——(1989) "Active investors, LBOs and the privatization of bankruptcy," *Journal of Applied Corporate Finance*, 2, 1: 35–44.

——(1991) "Corporate control and the politics of finance," *Journal of Applied Corporate Finance*, 4, 2: 13–33.

Jensen, M. C. and Meckling, W. H. (1976) "Theory of the firm: managerial behavior, agency costs and ownership structure," *Journal of Financial Economics*, 3, 1–4: 305–60.

Joskow, P. L. (1988) "Asset specificity and the structure of vertical relationships: empirical evidence," *Journal of Law, Economics and Organization*, 4, 1: 95–117

Kaplan, S. N. (1988) "Sources of value in management buyouts," unpublished Ph.D. dissertation, Harvard University.

Kester, C. (1992) "Industrial groups as systems of contractual governance," *Oxford Review of Economic Policy*, 8, 3: 24–44.

Klein, B., Crawford, R. G. and Alchian, A. A. (1978) "Vertical integration, appropriable rents and the competitive contracting process," *Journal of Law and Economics*, 21, 2: 297–326.

Kohler, K. (1991) "Inside information in mergers and acquisitions including leveraged buy-outs – a German viewpoint," in K. J. Hopt and E. Wymeersch (eds) *European Insider Dealing*, London: Butterworths, 263–71.

Kraus, A. and Stoll, H. (1972) "Price impacts of block trading on the New York Stock Exchange," *Journal of Finance*, 27, 3: 569–88.

Kreps, D. M. (1990) *A Course in Microeconomic Theory*, Hertfordshire: Harvester Wheatsheaf.

Krümmel, H. J. (1980) "German universal banking scrutinized," *Journal of Banking and Finance*, 4, 1: 33–55.

Lachmann, L. M. (1956) *Capital and its Structure*, Kansas City: Sheed Andrews & McMeel.

Leland, H. E. and Pyle, D. H. (1977) "Information asymmetries, financial structure and financial intermediation," *Journal of Finance*, 32, 2: 371–87.

LeRoy, S. (1989) "Efficient capital markets and martingales," *Journal of Economic Literature*, 27, 4: 1583–621.

Long, W. F. and Ravenscraft, D. J. (1991) "The record of LBO performance," in A. W. Sametz (ed.) *The Battle for Corporate Control: Shareholder Rights, Stakeholder Interests and Managerial Responsibilities*, Homewood, NJ: Irwin, 517–41.

Lorie, J. H. and Niederhoffer, V. (1974) "Predictive and statistical properties of insider trading," *Journal of Law and Economics*, 11, 1: 35–51.

Maddala, G. S. (1983) *Limited-Dependent and Qualitative Variables in Econometrics*, New York: Cambridge University Press.

Malkiel, B. (1987) "Efficient market hypothesis," in J. Eatwell, M. Milgate and P. Newman (eds) *The New Palgrave: A Dictionary of Economics*, vol. 2, London: Macmillan, 120–3.

Mandelker, G. and Raviv, A. (1977) "Investment banking: an economic analysis of optimal underwriting contracts," *Journal of Finance*, 32, 3: 683–94.

Manne, H. (1966) *Insider Trading and the Stock Market*, New York: Free Press.

Marshall, A. (1948) *Principles of Economics*, 8th ed., New York: Macmillan.

McGurn, P. S., Pampetito, S. and Spector, A. B. (1989) *State Takeover Laws*, Washington: Investor Responsibility Center.

Meyer, C. H. (1934) *The Securities Exchange Act of 1934*, New York: Francis Emory Fitch.

Monopolkommission (1978) *Hauptgutachten II: Fortschreitende Konzentration bei Grossunternehmen*, Baden-Baden: Nomos.

Myers, S. C. (1977) "Determinants of corporate borrowing," *Journal of Financial Economics*, 5, 2: 147–75.

Nakamura, L. I. (1991) "Commercial bank information," Federal Reserve Bank of Philadelphia Research Working Paper 92-1.

Nakatani, I. (1984) "The economic role of financial corporate grouping," in M. Aoki (ed.) *The economic Analysis of the Japanese Firm*, Amsterdam: North-Holland, 227–58.

Niehans, J. (1978) *The Theory of Money*, Baltimore: Johns Hopkins University Press.

Patinkin, D. (1965) *Money, Interest and Prices: An Integration of Monetary and Value Theory*, 2nd ed., New York: Harper & Row.

Pennacchi, G. G. (1988) "Loan sales and the cost of bank capital," *Journal of Finance*, 43, 2: 375–96.

Picot, A. (1981) "Der Beitrag der Theorie der Verfügungsrechte zur ökonomischen Analyse von Unternehmensverfassungen," in K. Bohr, J. Drukarczyk, H. J. Drumm and G. Scherrer (eds) *Unternehmensverfassung als Problem der Betriebswirtschaftslehre*, Berlin: Schmidt, 153–97.

Prowse, S. D. (1990) "Institutional investment patterns and corporate financial behavior in the United States and Japan," *Journal of Financial Economics*, 27, 1: 43–66.

——(1992) "The structure of corporate ownership in Japan," *Journal of Finance*, 47, 3: 1121–40.

Ramakrishnan, R. T. S. and Thakor, A. V. (1984) "Information reliability and a theory of financial intermediation," *Review of Economic Studies*, 51, 3: 415–32.

Rappaport, A. (1986) *Creating Shareholder Value: The New Standard for Business Performance*, New York: Free Press.

Reilly, F. K. (1985) *Investment Analysis and Portfolio Management*, New York: Dryden Press.

Rock, K. (1986) "Why new issues are underpriced," *Journal of Financial Economics*, 15, 1–2: 187–212.

Roe, M. J. (1990) "Political and legal restraints on ownership and control of public companies," *Journal of Financial Economics*, 27, 7–41.

——(1994) *Strong Managers, Weak Owners: The Political Roots of American Corporate Finance*, Princeton NJ: Princeton University Press.

Rudolph, B. (1993) "Capital requirements of German banks and the European Community proposals on banking supervision," in J. Dermine (ed.) *European Banking in the 1990s*, 2nd ed., Cambridge, MA: Blackwell, 373–85.

Schmidt, H. (1984) "Disclosure, insider information and capital market functions," in K. J. Hopt and G. Teubner (eds) *Corporate Governance and Directors' Liabilities: Legal, Economical and Sociological Analysis on Corporate Social Responsibility*, Berlin: deGruyter, 338–53.

Schmidt, R. H. and Terberger, E. (1996) *Grundzüge der Investitions- und Finanzierungstheorie*, 3rd ed., Wiesbaden: Gabler.

Schneider, H., Hellwig, H.-J. and Kingsman, D. J. (1978) *The German Banking System*, Frankfurt a.M.: Knapp.

Seyhun, N. H. (1986) "Insiders' profits, costs of trading and market efficiency," *Journal of Financial Economics*, 16, 2: 189–212.

Sheard, P. (1989a) "The main bank system and corporate monitoring and control in Japan," *Journal of Economic Behavior and Organization*, 11, 3: 399–422.

——(1989b) "The Japanese general trading company as an aspect of interfirm risk-sharing," *Journal of the Japanese and International Economies*, 3, 3: 308–22.

Shleifer, A. and Vishny, R. (1986) "Large shareholders and corporate control," *Journal of Political Economy*, 94, 3, Part 1: 461–88.

Simon, H. A. (1957) *Models of Man: Social and Rational. Mathematical Essays on Relational Human Behavior in a Social Setting*, New York: Wiley.

Smith, C. W. Jr (1986) "Investment banking and the capital acquisition process," *Journal of Financial Economics*, 15, 1–2: 3–29.

Smith, C. W. Jr and Warner, J. B. (1979) "On financial contracting: an analysis of bond covenants," *Journal of Financial Economics*, 7, 2: 117–61.

Spence, M. (1973) "Job market signaling," *Quarterly Journal of Economics*, 87, 3: 355–74.

——(1974) *Market Signaling: Informational Transfer in Hiring and Related Screening Processes*, Cambridge, MA: Harvard University Press.

Stiglitz, J. E. (1975a) "The theory of 'screening,' education and the distribution of wealth," *American Economic Review*, 65, 3: 283–300.

——(1975b) "Information and economic analysis," in M. Parkin and A. R. Nobay (eds) *Current Economic Problems*, Cambridge: Cambridge University Press, 27–52.

——(1985) "Capital markets and the control of capital," *Journal of Money, Credit and Banking*, 17, 2: 133–52.

Stiglitz, J. E. and Weiss, A. (1981) "Credit rationing in markets with imperfect information," *American Economic Review*, 71, 3: 393–410.

——(1983) "Incentive effects of termination: applications to the credit and labor markets," *American Economic Revue*, 73, 5: 912–27.

——(1985) "Credit rationing with collateral," Bell Communications Research Inc., Economics Discussion Papers: 12.

——(1987a) "Credit rationing: reply," *American Economic Review*, 77, 1: 228–31.

——(1987b) "Macroeconomic equilibrium and credit rationing," NBER Working Paper no. 2164.

Tobin, J. (1965) "The theory of portfolio selection," in F. H. Hahn and F. P. R. Brechling (eds) *The Theory of Interest Rates*, London: Macmillan, 3–51.

Toyo Keizai Shinpo Sha (1995) *Kigyo Keiretsu Soran '95*, Tokyo: Toyo Keizai Shinpo Sha.

US Securities and Exchange Commission (1963) *Report of Special Study of Securities Markets, Part 4*, Washington: US Government Printing Office.

——(1966) *Public Policy Implication of Investment Company Growth*, Washington: US Government Printing Office.

Wenger, E. (1992) "Universalbanken und Depotstimmrecht," in H. Görner (ed.) *Der Markt für Unternnehmenskontrollen*, Berlin: Duncker & Humblot, 73–103.

Wharton School of Finance and Commerce (1962) *A Study of Mutual Funds*, Washington: US Government Printing Office.

Williamson, O. E. (1979) "Transaction-cost economics: the governance of contractual relations," *Journal of Law and Economics*, 22, 2: 233–61.

——(1981) "The modern corporation: origins, evolution, attributes," *Journal of Economic Literature*, 19, 4: 1537–68.

——(1983) "Credible commitments: using hostages to support exchange," *American Economic Review*, 73, 4: 519–40.

——(1985) *The Economic Institutions of Capitalism: Firms, Markets, Relational Contracting*, New York: Free Press.

——(1996) *The Mechanisms of Governance*, New York: Oxford University Press.

Williamson, O. E. and Bhargava, N. (1972) "Assessing and classifying the internal structure and control apparatus of the modern corporation," in K. Cowling (ed.) *Market Structure and Corporate Behavior Theory and Empirical Analysis of the Firm*, London: Gray-Mills, 125–48.

World Bank (1989) *World Development Report 1989*, New York: Oxford University Press.

Zavoina, W. and McKelvey, R. D. (1975) "A Statistical model for the analysis of ordinal level dependent variables," *Journal of Mathematical Sociology*, 4, 1: 103–20.

Zeckhauser, R. and Pound, J. (1990) "Are large shareholders effective monitors? An investigation of share ownership and corporate performance," in R. G. Hubbard (ed.) *Asymmetric Information, Corporate Finance and Investment*, Chicago: University of Chicago Press, 149–80.

NAME INDEX

SUBJECT INDEX